Elvis

Elvis

memories and memorabilia

RICHARD BUSKIN

a Salamander book

Published by Salamander Books Limited
LONDON

A Salamander book

Published by Salamander Books Ltd.,
129–137 York Way
London N7 9LG
United Kingdom

9 8 7 6 5 4 3 2 1

© Salamander Books 1995

Distributed by Random House Value Publishing, Inc.
40 Engelhard Avenue
Avenel, New Jersey 07001

A CIP catalog record for this book is available from the
Library of Congress.

ISBN 0-517-14032-2

CREDITS
Editor: Krystyna Zukowska
Designer: Mark Holt
Memorabilia Photography: Jonathan Pollock (UK
photography) and John Freeman (Holland and
Germany). © Salamander Books Ltd.
Colour reproduction: Pixel Tech Prepress Pte Ltd.
Singapore

Printed in Spain

ACKNOWLEDGMENTS

The Publishers wish to thank Ger Rijff in Amsterdam,
Andreas Schröer and Jürgen Keilwerth in Germany and
Michael Haywood in England for allowing Salamander
Books Ltd to photograph items from their extensive
collections of Elvis memorabilia, and for their help and
advice throughout the project. The Publishers would
also like to thank Will Steeds, who originally thought
up the idea for this book.

The Publishers have endeavored to ensure that both
the still photographs and the artifacts in this book are
correctly credited. Should any illustration in this book
be incorrectly attributed, the Publishers apologize.

Front endpaper: Elvis fans greeting their hero in Miami

Back endpaper: Elvis performing live in 1956 at an
annual concert in Tupelo, Mississippi

Page 2: Elvis during his special satellite performance
'Aloha from Hawaii'

Page 4: Elvis on stage in Florida, 1955

contents

elvis

In the beginning there was the sneer, that curled upper lip and the heavy-lidded stare. Then there were the long sideburns and greased back hair, the arrogant stance and the garish flair. *Nobody* looked like Elvis Presley. No one had that lopsided grin, those smouldering eyes, the air of primitive sexuality and that charisma, all rolled into one dynamic package. Back in the mid-Fifties nobody dressed the way he did, no one sang quite like him and none of his peers captivated their audiences in anything even approaching the same manner. The looks, the talent, the personality - even the name was unique. ELVIS. An ad man's dream, similar to Garbo, except that in her case the name was a film-star fabrication. His wasn't. The man really did have it all.

Sam Phillips had opened the Memphis Recording Service in January 1950 in order to provide black artists with a receptive environment in which to record blues and gospel music. It was, however, his quest for 'something different', or, more to the point, a white artist capable of conveying the feel of black music to racially intolerant American audiences, which in the summer of 1954 convinced him to invest time and money in a strange-looking nineteen-year-old truck driver.

Elvis' flamboyant performing style may have been influenced by impassioned Pentecostal church preachers and the blues artists in the clubs on Beale Street in

Left: *Elvis '56 - mean, moody and oozing raw sex appeal, courtesy of those wild sideburns, smouldering eyes and pouting lips. This was the year that it all happened for the 21-year-old former truck driver - TV notoriety, chart success and a Hollywood contract, so what more could he ask for? Perhaps some black hair dye for those blond roots?*

'The image is one thing and the human being is another. It's very hard to live up to an image.'
Elvis Presley, 1972.

Memphis, yet he crooned more like his idol Dean Martin and boasted that, 'I don't sound like nobody'. Now Phillips decided to satisfy his curiosity as to 'what this damned fool could do', and the results, as Sam himself later recalled, were 'all I've ever looked for in my entire life.' Memphis DJ, Dewey Phillips (no relation), spun the 'B' side of Presley's first single, *That's All Right (Mama)*, on his *Red, Hot and Blue* radio show at 9.30 pm on Saturday, July 10, 1954, and he was obliged to break in over Scotty Moore's guitar solo to inform Southern listeners that the singer was, in fact, a white boy.

In truth, however, Elvis did not really sound like the black artists of that time as much as he captured their feel - the urgency in the voice, the toying with phrases, the sexual overtones. When he moaned, *'I need your lovin','* he clearly wasn't just referring to a spot of kissing and holding hands. He meant business, and the titles of many of his early songs clearly conveyed this: *Baby Let's Play House*, *One Night*, *A Big Hunk O' Love*, *Doncha' Think It's Time*, *I Need Your Love Tonight* - these were viewed as blunt and earthy during an era when other, more 'acceptable' songs about teenage love and angst boasted titles such as *Angel Baby*, *Sixteen Candles*, *Young Love*, *At The Hop* and *Graduation Day*.

Good, clean fun they might have been, but Elvis apparently had no time for singing about the pleasantries of high-school dates and growing up. He already had plenty of experience under his belt and he was now only interested in getting down to basics - in other words, s-e-x, albeit still by implication, but fairly heavy implication all the same.

Of course, Elvis did not write his own hit material, and, while some of it was composed specifically for him, much was not, but this did not matter. For, courtesy of his unrivalled vocal ability to infuse a song with tenderness (as on *Young and Beautiful*), aggression (*Trouble*), soulfulness (*I Want You, I Need You, I Love You*), exuberance (*Got A Lot O' Livin' To Do!*), self-pity (*Heartbreak Hotel*) or humor (*All Shook Up*), he could turn any number into whatever he wanted it to mean. *Good Rockin' Tonight* was a 1948 R&B dance hit for its composer, Roy Brown, but six years later, as performed on stage and committed to tape by the nineteen-year-old Presley, it became, in the words of country music critic Nick Tosches, 'not merely a party song but an invitation to a holocaust'. *'We're gonna rock, rock, rock, rock,'* Elvis rhythmically announces as Bill Black pounds out the backing on his upright bass, and by way of the urgency in his voice and the suggestiveness of his phrasing it is clear that he is in no way

Right: *Beale Street in Memphis as it looks today. It was in the blues clubs located here that, in the early-50's, Elvis was heavily influenced by the performing style and vocal delivery of many of the black artists.*

elvis

singing about some straightforward jiving at the high school hop.

For teenagers around the American South in 1954 and 1955, and then the rest of the country and much of the world thereafter, this was like a call to arms. The Second World War was now a part of history and these post-war youths were looking for excitement, yet, while many of them had more money in their pockets than their predecessors, there was a growing feeling that there was little of worth to spend it on.

Bored with the staid customs of its forebears - with the carefully groomed screen, radio and recording idols, the strictly adhered-to establishment guidelines and the restrictive tradition that required young people to be 'seen but not heard' - the 'war baby' generation was just waiting for the chance to break free and establish its own code of conduct. Moreover, these children were no longer prepared to conform to a world run by aged politicians - President Eisenhower on one side of the Atlantic, Prime Ministers Churchill and Eden on the other - who talked publicly about peace but nevertheless felt obliged to participate in the escalating nuclear arms race.

Rebellion was in the air, and when, in 1955, Bill Haley and the Comets' *Rock Around The Clock* was played over the opening credits of that classic juvenile delinquency film, *The Blackboard Jungle*, youngsters immediately latched onto the upbeat rockabilly music. However, the song's pudgy, kiss-curled performer looked more like a father figure than a teen idol, and what with his tartan jacket and ready smile he desperately lacked the sensuality and charisma that could fire the kids' collective imagination. No, there had to be someone better suited to their needs.

James Dean had just such qualities, his Brando-esque sullenness and general air of nonconformity perfectly summing up the feelings of disaffected youth. But, while the actor's fatal 1955 car crash at the age of just 24 guaranteed him instant immortality, he left behind - in the words of the *Picture Post* of October 8, 1956 - 'millions of teenage rebels heading for nowhere, some in "hot rod" cars, others on the

'Before Elvis there was nothing. Without him there would have been no Beatles.'
Jonn Lennon, 1977.

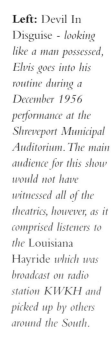

Left: Devil In Disguise - *looking like a man possessed, Elvis goes into his routine during a December 1956 performance at the Shreveport Municipal Auditorium. The main audience for this show would not have witnessed all of the theatrics, however, as it comprised listeners to the* Louisiana Hayride *which was broadcast on radio station KWKH and picked up by others around the South.*

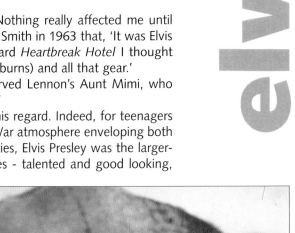
blare of rock 'n' roll music, some with guns in their hands. And at their head - a dead leader.'

The time was ripe for Elvis Aaron Presley.

John Lennon, who would later admit that, 'Nothing really affected me until Elvis,' told *New Musical Express* interviewer Alan Smith in 1963 that, 'It was Elvis who got me hooked for beat music. When I heard *Heartbreak Hotel* I thought "this is it," and I started to grow sideboards (sideburns) and all that gear.'

'He became a mess, almost overnight,' observed Lennon's Aunt Mimi, who raised him, 'and all because of Elvis Presley, I say.'

However, John Lennon was hardly alone in this regard. Indeed, for teenagers everywhere, especially those enduring the Cold War atmosphere enveloping both the United States and Europe during the mid-Fifties, Elvis Presley was the larger-than-life embodiment of all their wildest fantasies - talented and good looking, while oozing sex appeal, rebellion, charm and aggression in equal proportions. Here he was, the real thing; liberation!

For years, America's white racist extremists had been screaming at their kids not to buy those licentious 'negro records' - or 'race music' as the genre was commonly referred to - with their 'vulgar lyrics' and 'savage rhythms'. It was forbidden to even listen to them, but many kids did, secretly tuning in to small black-music radio stations in their rooms late at night. There they heard the raw instrumentals, the wailing voices and all of those suggestive references to 'primitive urges'; indeed, natural urges, but ones which young white Americans were not permitted to talk about.

The advent of Elvis Presley therefore heralded a new kind of hero - someone who was doing all of the talking for them - and those concerned parents, those church leaders, those small-minded politicians and outright racists couldn't even blame it on the fact that he was black. Certainly, his influences came partly from that direction, but there was no denying that this was a white guy, right from the blue of his eyes to the reddish auburn of his hair

Right: *Hillbilly Baby - who would have believed that this innocent- looking 2-year-old, born into extreme poverty, would grow up to become the symbol of, first, teen rebellion, and then later on, showbiz glitz and glamor? Still, there is already a lost look in those eyes, the upper lip is curling nicely and that hat is a knockout.*

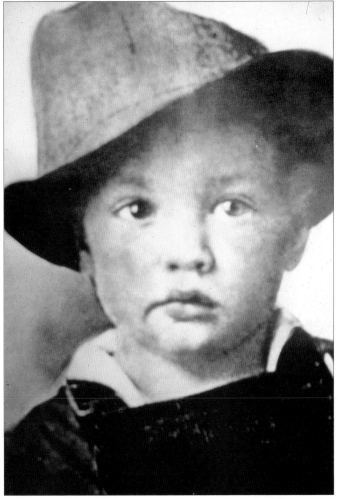

elvis

Above: *The boy who would be king - aged about 15, and our hero's natural charms already appear to be having an impact on Memphis' female contingent, if the lovestruck expression on young Betty McMahan's face is anything to go by.*

> **'Elvis was a country boy, but the way they had him living they never turned off the air conditioning. Took away all the good air. You get sick from that.'**
>
> *James Brown, 1977.*

(although later he would intensify his looks by dying it jet black). He was, in fact, the all-American boy, but one with attitude!

In truth, however, the man and the image did not always tread the same path, for as with many figures who have fame or notoriety thrust upon them, it was not so much a case of what Elvis Presley did as of what he was perceived to have done and represent that caused all the furore.

The second of twins born to Vernon and Gladys Presley on January 8, 1935, (the other, Jesse Garon, was stillborn), Elvis spent his early life in the Deep South town of Tupelo, Mississippi, accustomed to the deprivations of poverty and the comforting surroundings of The First Assembly Church of God. There he learned not only to move with the rhythmic swaying of the little congregation, but also to have a deep respect for God and family and to be courteous to his elders. Thus, the same man who was charged with - and subsequently acquitted of - assaulting a Memphis filling station manager in October 1956, could more often than not be heard addressing whoever he encountered as either 'Sir' of 'Ma'am'; and that same irreverent lunatic who appeared to be possessed by Lucifer himself on the *Milton Berle Show* was also capable of releasing an album solely dedicated to the music of the Lord.

Therefore, while Elvis was gaining notoriety throughout the latter half of the 1950s, and respectable, squeaky-clean Pat Boone was doing his best to emasculate songs by the likes of Little Richard in order to make them more palatable to a white audience, the two men's fundamental beliefs were, in reality, not all that dissimilar. Because, as his later career would serve to prove, at heart Elvis Presley was never really very much of a rebel. While introducing white America to the raunchy music of Arthur 'Big Boy' Crudup he aspired to be a big balladeer, and there is good cause to believe that underlying everything was his ambition to be a popular actor, combining the sullen qualities of Brando and Dean with the smooth good looks and all-round charm of Tony Curtis.

These were the goals which Elvis clearly had in mind when, in March 1960, he emerged from an honourable and highly-publicised two-year stint in the army. Yet, while a succession of badly scripted (if profitable) movies and increasingly indifferent song material managed, by the mid-60s, to all but destroy the massive influence which he once had, the name of Elvis Presley still spelled magic in the minds of millions; a star among stars, and a reminder - despite his own taming - of how exciting things had once been for the first true rock 'n' roll generation.

Right: *Gone are the sideburns and the hairgrease, replaced by the smooth, well-groomed looks of an early '60's matinée idol. Elvis, circa 1963, about to lose touch with the contemporary music scene.*

When, therefore, Elvis did return to form towards the end of the decade, following up a landmark TV show with some wonderful new recordings and his first live concerts in eight years, it was almost as if his legions of fans were willing him to succeed, and, for a time, he did not disappoint them.

The all-new Elvis who ended the 1960s on a high and started the 1970s with his career completely rejuvenated had an altogether different persona from the hip, swaggering, flashy young character of thirteen or so years before. Now he was the consumate all-round entertainer, his looks carefully groomed, his stage movements more precisely choreographed, his very presence much more contrived. Still, people of all ages and from all corners of the Earth lined up in their hundreds of thousands to see him perform throughout the United States, for that was still the only country where he did perform. And, even when his own enthusiasm for life eventually began to dry up, when the originality and innovation disappeared from his concerts, his once lithe figure turned to fat, his health gave out and Elvis became something of a parody of the man he had once been, the fans still adored him - and they do to this day.

In the final analysis, Elvis Presley was a superstar in the purest sense; a superstar before that word had even been incorporated into the English language. His only rivals in the popular music stakes were The Beatles, and during their halcyon years they enjoyed even more widespread adulation than Presley - one reason

11

elvis

being that they at least toured overseas. Yet their image was firmly rooted in that of the 'boys-next-door'; more straightforward, more realistic and down-to-earth. Elvis, on the other hand, immersed himself in the image and lifestyle that he and his manager, Colonel Tom Parker, had crafted; that of a star-spangled, pampered and protected individual who regularly emerged from his private kingdom in order to bestow his greatness upon the masses: self-mocking yet magnificent, accessible yet out of reach.

During the latter phase of Elvis' life this grand existence was elevated to almost messianic proportions, and it was often difficult for the public at large to see him for the country boy that he still was under all of the glitz and glamor. When The Beatles grew tired of constantly smiling for the cameras and turning on the charm for the press and media they dispensed with their glossy, boys-next-door 'mop top' image. They grew long hair, behaved more outrageously and, as a result,

Below: *The end is near as Elvis pours out his heart and soul for a rendition of* My Way *during a concert in Omaha on 19 June 1977. Just over seven weeks later the King of Rock 'n' Roll would be dead.*

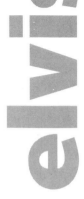

elvis

'There's no way to measure the impact he made on society or the void that he leaves.'
Pat Boone, 1977.

were later able to resume something approaching a more stable and private lifestyle.

Elvis, on the other hand, was never able to lead anything like a normal life after he found fame and fortune in 1956, and he quickly fell into a routine of partying at night, sleeping by day, shopping at especially-opened stores at three in the morning and hiring cinemas or entire fairgrounds whenever he fancied visiting them with friends. These associates, of course, were a select bunch who came to be known as the 'Memphis Mafia'; a collection of buddies, lackeys and yes-men who were prepared to do everything for The King at his court. If Elvis' cup needed filling he did not need to ask; if he wanted company at any time of the day or night somebody was there for him; and, if he cracked a joke, everyone laughed.

No doubt, Elvis must have felt smothered by this kind of setup after the initial novelty had worn off, yet at the same time he apparently did not want to divest himself of a regime and lifestyle that only served to reaffirm his own importance. Likewise, dealing alone with the burden of fame must have been infinitely more difficult than it was for The Beatles as a group. Yet, while Elvis could have chosen to leave it all behind in much the same way that they did, the simple truth must be that he did not want to. He loved the fans' adulation and they in turn loved him for it.

Elvis' life was one characterized by hard-to-break habits - the cycle of films, the incessant concert tours and the increasing dependency on prescription drugs. Yet it was also a life which fulfilled many fantasies for both the man and his followers, and while the god-like status was plainly too much for one human being to cope with, it is a testament to Elvis' special talent and unique personality that he nevertheless managed to carry it off. Indeed, it is likely that, even without all of the fame and fortune, he would have still had the natural presence to turn heads whenever he walked into a room.

'When I was a boy I was the hero in comic books and movies,' Elvis Presley said in later years. 'I grew up believing in that dream. Now I've lived it out. That's all a man can ask for.'

Left: *A paunchy and tired-looking Elvis pictured in 1976 with Linda Thompson, his main girlfriend after the divorce from Priscilla. Reflecting on his privacy-seeking routine of starting the day at sunset, Linda would later state that 'life with Elvis meant living like a bat.'*

13

the fifties' concerts : good rockin' tonight

Picture the scene: the curtains part and out walks this guy, six feet tall with long, greased-back hair and sideburns, wearing a green jacket, red trousers, a pink shirt, pink socks and white 'buck' shoes. He has a sneer on his face, an insolent look in his mascara-lashed, heavy-lidded eyes, and as he steps into the spotlight he leans forward, legs apart, and grabs the mike stand with his right hand. The guitar, more a weapon than an instrument, hangs loose as he raises his other arm above his head, gazes moodily out at the audience and howls, 'We-e-e-ell...'. There is instant hysteria.

The venue could be anywhere, from Russwood Park in Memphis to the Gator Bowl in Jacksonville, Florida, and the song one of many which are embellished with this standard gospel-like intro during the early years of rock 'n' roll - *That's All Right (Mama)*, *Good Rockin' Tonight*, *I Got A Woman* and *Heartbreak Hotel*, to name but a few. The whole routine serves to tease, and it places the paying punters right

16▷

'If I stand still while I'm singing, I'm dead, man.
I might as well go back to driving a truck.'

Elvis Presley, 1956.

Right: *A 1956 poster, capitalizing on the vibrant Presley image and his earliest TV appearances, whilst helpfully informing people that Elvis was, in fact, the star of his own show.*

Right: *Three 'flasher' badges from 1956, showing how Elvis could shake that pelvis, play his guitar and curl that lip.*

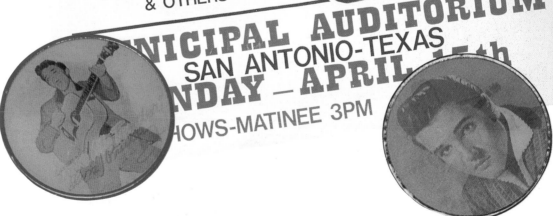

THE ELVIS PRESLEY SHOW

STARRING
IN PERSON

ELVIS PRESLEY

WITH THE BLUE MOON BOYS
THE FARMER BOYS
WANDA JACKSON
HANK LOCKLIN
CHARLIE WALKER MC
& OTHERS

NOW APPEARING AS GUEST STAR ON THE JACKIE GLEASON TELEVISION SHOW

NICIPAL AUDITORIUM
SAN ANTONIO-TEXAS
NDAY — APRIL 15th
HOWS-MATINEE 3PM

Left: *Tempt 'n' tease was a game which Elvis excelled at right from the start, straddling the footlights as he encouraged the hysterical girls to reach out and touch, and then stepping back just before the going got a little too rough.*

Right: *This collectors' plate commemorates Elvis returning to his birthplace of Tupelo on 25 September 1956 to perform one more time at the annual Mississippi- Alabama State Fair and Dairy Show, where he had first taken to the stage as a 10 year old.*

where the artist wants them, in the palm of his hand.

Now his right leg begins to shake, and, as the song progresses, he starts to roll his groin and thrust his hips back and forth in the most suggestive manner possible. At other times he moans, sways, falls to one knee or gyrates his pelvis in a 'bump 'n' grind' motion that would not shame a stripper. He is like a man possessed, the Devil incarnate, and the girls in the audience are nearly beside themselves with the excitement of it all. For them, this has got to be the closest they'll ever get to sex without experiencing the real thing.

Presley in the Fifties - The Hillbilly Cat, the Memphis Flash, the Nation's First Atomic-Powered Singer, or, as the press and media quickly dubbed him, Elvis the Pelvis. A taste of freedom for America's restless post-war teenagers and the ultimate threat to those who wanted to keep them in their place. Here was Marlon Brando with a guitar!

'When I stand still, I'm dead,' Elvis asserted in 1956. 'People say I'm vulgar. They say I use my hips disgustingly. But that's my way of putting over a song. I have to move.'

He was almost telling the truth, for, in the beginning at least, Elvis did move spontaneously to the music when he was performing; shaking his legs, swivelling his shoulders and tilting his head back, eyes closed. This was all in the best Southern gospel tradition, of course, but a little sex was also thrown

in for good measure. Almost immediately the girls in the audience began to respond, and Elvis, a naturally astute showman, was not slow to capitalize on the opportunity.

'I really stumbled onto something,' Presley admitted in 1972, when recalling his first big concert appearance at the Overton Park Shell in Memphis, on July 30, 1954. 'Everyone in the audience was hollering and shouting and generally going crazy and I didn't know why. I was dumbfounded. Kinda bewildered. It wasn't until I came off that I knew the reason. It was because I had been wriggling and shaking and writhing. So in my encore I wriggled and twisted more - and the more I did, the wilder the audience became.'

In other words, Elvis did not have to move to the music as much as it paid him to do so. Indeed, by the time of his first national TV appearance, on the January 28, 1956 live broadcast of Jackie Gleason's *Stage Show*, some of his gyrations were clearly contrived for maximum audience effect. Things, however, had not always been this way.

Throughout his life Elvis was basically a shy person whose two main forms of expression were his public performances and his flashy image. The first instance of the former took place when, at around the age of ten, he took to the stage of the annual Mississippi-Alabama State Fair and Dairy Show and sang the popular Red Foley tear-jerker, *Old Shep*. Elvis scooped the $5 second prize for his effort that day (which was broadcast live over Tupelo radio station WELO), and for his eleventh birthday Ma and Pa Presley bought their son a cheap guitar. Elvis would have preferred a

17

Above: *The Memphis Flash struts his stuff - call the police and lock up your daughters!*

Right: *Even this sheet music was adorned with those digusting antics...*

bicycle or a rifle. The bike was too expensive. The gun was too dangerous. The rest is history.

Soon, having been taught to play guitar by his father's brother Vester, Elvis carried the instrument wherever he went and sang to whoever would listen; at cafés, bars, parties or just in front of the Presley home. Then, during his last year at L.C. Humes High School in Memphis (to where the family had moved when he was thirteen), Elvis began entertaining his classmates, and he took first prize there in the annual variety show when he performed *Old Shep*, as well as an encore of - according to various reports - either *Cold Cold Icy Fingers* or *Till I Waltz Again With You*.

Buoyed by this success, Elvis next began hanging around some of the local musicians, and, after graduating from Humes in the summer of 1953, he occasionally sang with a newly-formed gospel quartet named The Songfellows. In October of that year he was also introduced on stage by DJ Dewey Phillips at the Eagle's Nest club, a country swing joint which was located on the outskirts of Memphis. Here, during an intermission, he sang Dean Martin's then-current hit, *That's Amore*: 'When the moon hits your eye like a big pizza pie...' This may not have been the stuff of teenage rebellion, but then this was just a sign of things to come much later in Elvis' career.

During the next nine months there were stints working in a military tools factory and then driving a truck for Crown Electric, prior to Elvis having his first single released on the Sun Records label and performing at the Overton Park Shell. Bottom of the bill in a lineup

Left: *Going to the show? Then what better way to take some goodies with you than in this smart Elvis overnight bag!*

Below: *Portrait of the artist as a young punk: hip gear, a cocky smile and a swaggering stance - any clues as to what created a stir back in 1954?*

headed by country yodeller Slim Whitman, Elvis had only been included by local DJ Bob Neal as a favor to Sun's owner, Sam Phillips.

The newcomer's main task was to warm up the audience for the next act on stage, Webb Pierce, and during the matinée performance he barely managed to achieve this by crooning *Old Shep* and *That's When Your Heartaches Begin*. Afterwards, Bob Neal advised Elvis that, for the evening show, he should steer clear of the country ballads which he naturally gravitated towards (in terms of personal preference if not natural ability), in favour of some more upbeat material. Elvis took the hint and the startling results were etched in the memories of all who saw him at around this time, including Paul Lichter, who, in his book, *The Boy Who Dared To Rock*, recalled:

19

'The curtains parted and, standing on centre stage, Elvis was a sight to behold. He wore a black sport coat trimmed with pink darts and black high rise pants that featured pink pocket flaps and pink lightning bolts lining the outside seam of the leg. He threw one arm above his head and began to move his leg in the now famous corkscrew motion, his smouldering blue eyes peering out at the audience, his thick lips curled into a sexy snarl. He hadn't sung his first note and they were already screaming.'

By the time that Elvis had finished his set and left the stage he hadn't so much warmed up the paying punters as set them on fire. Meanwhile, Webb Pierce was furious, and after shouting some obscenities at the nineteen-year-old upstart he walked out of the show. Clearly, this could not continue. Soon, Elvis would be topping his own bill.

In the meantime, the budding 'King of Western Bop' did not feel financially secure enough to quit driving a truck until November 1954. Thereafter, one of the earliest known live recordings of Elvis captures him performing at a show in Gladewater, Texas, on December 18 of that year, backed by Scotty Moore on guitar, Bill Black on bass, Jimmy Day on steel guitar and Floyd Cramer on piano. Listening today it is evident that the girls in the audience already screamed whenever Elvis raised his voice (and, presumably, shook his legs), and by the time of a concert at the Eagle's Hall in Houston, Texas, in March 1955, the 'Bopping Hillbilly' (as he was introduced) was displaying all of the cocky, streetwise self-confidence that would soon come to characterize some of his early movie roles.

Towards the end of the recording we hear Elvis return for an encore: 'Thank you very much,' he says to the audience of around 150 people. 'I was coming back anyway... I'd like to do a little song right here that I hope you

Far left: *Las Vegas, 1956: Elvis gives a far more honest appraisal of the situation than either D.J.' Scotty or Bill.*

Left: *Cool, calm and collected on the Louisiana Hayride, December 1956, yet liable to cut loose at any time.*

Above: *Between 19 July 1954 and 1 August 1955, Elvis had five singles released on the Sun Records label. Each of these paired a country song on one side with an R&B number on the other, and, to many, they were Presley's best ever recordings. Now they are collectors' items.*

21

people like... This one's called *"Little darlin', you broke my heart when you went away, but I'll break your jaw when you come back..."*.'

Even though this flip, macho attitude was adopted to impress the girls, it was also possibly Elvis' way of trying to fend off the glaring attentions of their frequently jealous boyfriends, many of whom would often resort to violent measures in order to reassert their own authority. For, as Elvis' reputation grew throughout the South during 1955, so did the hostility of local rednecks who wanted - and often attempted - to set upon and sort him out. The police helped to provide protection at shows, but soon it was necessary to resort to a team of full-time minders for round-the-clock security, and this was a precaution that Elvis - still barely out of his teens - would never dispense with.

Below: *A rare bronze plastic statuette from 1956, together with the original magazine advert with a photo of the man to force the point home. It was fair likeness, but Elvis's name was on the guitar just in case.*

In the meantime, while releasing a succession of moderately successful discs on the Sun label, Elvis, Scotty and Bill - or the Blue Moon Boys as they were now calling themselves - undertook an increasing number of personal appearances in order to help promote these recordings. With Bob Neal taking over the managerial reins and looking after bookings, more than 200 dates were performed within the space of a year; one-night stands all over the South, mainly as part of multi-star package shows headlined by country star Hank Snow.

These performances would typically take the form of Elvis going through his devil-possessed routine; leering, shaking, tempting, cajoling and generally causing a riot, while the impassive Scotty Moore concentrated on his guitar licks and the embullient Bill Black thumped his upright bass, occasionally

sat astride it and did his level best to help 'put on a show'. Just as typically, there would be pandemonium in the audience and, with increasing frequency, complaints from the police, local authorities and outraged parents.

Travelling by road from one venue to the next, Elvis was usually so wound up with nervous energy after each concert that Scotty, Bill and D.J. Fontana (who joined as drummer in the early spring of 1955) had to try and calm him down every night before they themselves could catch up with some sleep. Long walks, arm wrestling contests, anything would be attempted in order to wear him out, and, as if all of this wasn't enough, the busy schedule became even more frantic through 1956.

By then, as Presley's comet burst across the American skies, several shows a day had to be interspersed

with TV, radio, recording and film engagements. It was less than two years since Elvis had made his first professional recordings and concert appearances, yet he had mushroomed from a local unknown into a national institution, and this is a fact which is seldom emphasized. Indeed, others like The Beatles, who struggled through seven years and more than a thousand live performances before rising to prominence, were crawling along at a snail's pace by comparison.

Bob Neal's management contract with Elvis expired on 15 March 1956. Thereafter, seasoned manager, agent, promoter and all-round business-shark Colonel Tom Parker was directing operations, and, determined to ensure that every profit-related angle was being thoroughly exploited by his boy, he saw to it that kids up and down the country got to witness all of the fun first-hand.

Once *The Elvis Presley Show* had hit the road, the small clubs were replaced by large halls, arenas and ballparks, and these were reached by the star and his entourage in a fleet of brand new Cadillacs. Inside the venues, an assortment of variety acts - from jugglers to comedians - would have the unenviable task of trying to entertain several thousand manic teenagers whose only thoughts were centered on their hero. Predominantly female, these kids could feel the hysteria building up inside of them until they were fit to burst. Finally, the MC would announce the name of Elvis Presley, the man himself would stride onto the stage amid a barrage of popping flashbulbs, and out in the audience there would be a collective explosion of emotions.

Excitement, lust and frustration would express themselves in the form of fainting spells, sobs, moans and

Right: *Elvis, together with his manager Bob Neal (center-right) and booking agents Colonel Parker and Hank Snow, celebrates the buying-out of his Sun contract on 20 November 1955. Neal and Snow would not be smiling for long, however, for, thanks to the wily old Colonel, they would soon be cut out of the picture altogether.*

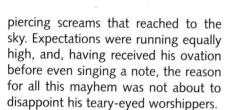

piercing screams that reached to the sky. Expectations were running equally high, and, having received his ovation before even singing a note, the reason for all this mayhem was not about to disappoint his teary-eyed worshippers.

In concert, Elvis' voice - alternately raw, melodic, rasping and growling - was easily as good as on the records, and in the flesh he looked every bit as handsome as in the magazines and on television. His stage movements, however, were something else. Unlike the tame publicity poses or often toned-down TV performances they were violent, aggressive, a veritable sexual assault on the senses. No wonder the moral saviours of the nation were all up in arms! This supposedly well-behaved Southern boy was blatantly out to corrupt the minds of their children, and he was doing so by straddling the mike stand, punching a fist in the air and thrusting his groin in their faces!

The police would often have to form a human chain in order to prevent the stir-crazy kids from rushing the stage, yet all the while they were also becoming more and more preoccupied with the disgusting antics of that madman with the microphone. In

24

Above: *If you couldn't actually meet Elvis in person, then wearing this official T-shirt was at least one way of feeling a little closer to your idol, while also contributing towards his next pink Cadillac!*

Right: *Police, bodyguards and an air of general mayhem surrounded Elvis at all of his concerts after 1955, but here our boy is either stressed or he has just swallowed his microphone.*

Left: *As not all of Elvis' concerts were staged indoors back in 1956, male fan could protect their elaborate pompadour hairstyles from the rain by donning this very trendy pork-pie hat.*

Below: *The girls, meanwhile, could scream, swoon and faint to their hearts' content, whilst knowing that not a hair would be out of place as long as they wore their stylish Elvis headscarves.*

25

Below: *Whilst outraged citizens were complaining about Elvis' below-the-waist wriggling, the* *manufacturers of this bookend easily ensured that he could cause no such offence. Problem solved!*

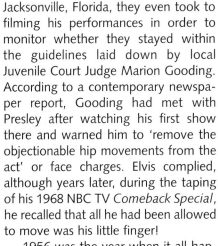

Jacksonville, Florida, they even took to filming his performances in order to monitor whether they stayed within the guidelines laid down by local Juvenile Court Judge Marion Gooding. According to a contemporary newspaper report, Gooding had met with Presley after watching his first show there and warned him to 'remove the objectionable hip movements from the act' or face charges. Elvis complied, although years later, during the taping of his 1968 NBC TV *Comeback Special*, he recalled that all he had been allowed to move was his little finger!

1956 was the year when it all happened for Elvis Presley. By the time that he played the Cotton Bowl in Dallas there were more than 25,000 fans in the audience, a ten-foot-high fence around the stage and a brand new white Lincoln convertible to transport the smiling, waving star straight onto the field. Things just kept going from good to better, but there had still been the odd setback along the way, and most notable amongst these was a pretty disastrous concert debut in, of all places, Las Vegas.

Initially headlining a fortnight's engagement at the New Frontier Hotel during late April and early May, Elvis had to suffer the indignity of being reduced to second-billing behind comedian Shecky Greene after the first few shows. The all-adult Vegas audiences, accustomed to the much smoother likes of Dean Martin or Frank Sinatra, were simply not yet ready for rock 'n' roll, and their polite applause were no substitute for the screams of adolescent girls.

One critic likened Elvis' performance to 'a jug of corn liquor at a champagne party,' while, during the show taped on May 6, the man himself commented, 'This makes our second week here, tonight's our last night and we've had a pretty hard time staying... uh, had a pretty good time while we're here. We've got a few little songs we'd like to do for you [that] we have on record, and our own style of singing, if you want to call it singing...'.

A rendition of *Long Tall Sally* ensued, followed by Elvis announcing, 'Thank you, music lovers'. He had made his point. It would be thirteen years before he would return to Las Vegas, and then, ironically, he would be making his comeback to live concerts and the story would be altogether different.

Meanwhile, having put this brief debacle firmly behind him, it was onwards and upwards for the man who would be king. 1957 rolled on, and with it a spring tour which gained much of its notoriety courtesy of the gold lamé suit which Elvis wore, designed by Nudie Cohen of Hollywood. Controversy followed Elvis wherever he played, from Chicago through the North-Eastern states and onto Toronto, Montreal and Ottawa, and thus the pattern was set for a similar three-week stint which commenced in August and took in the Pacific North-West.

Stadiums served as the venues, with flatbed trailers as the stages, and all ran fairly smoothly until a show in Vancouver on September 3, where fans climbed over barricades, rushed the stage and entered into bloody conflict with the police. The next day, Elvis was heavily criticized in the local press for inciting all of the trouble and then leav-

Right: When It Rains It Really Pours - *Elvis always put 100% effort into his '50's concert performances, leaving him physically and emotionally drained.*

Below: *The Colonel thoughtfully provided plenty of pencils and 'sticky pics' for those writing love letters to their idol. Now, where is that note paper?*

ing town, but still the Presley band-waggon thundered on, and by the time that he performed at the Pan-Pacific Auditorium in Los Angeles on October 28 and 29 of 1957, Elvis had reached the pinnacle of his career.

The soundtrack album from his second film, *Loving You*, was number one on the US album charts, *Jailhouse Rock* was about to top the singles charts and the film of the same name had people queuing up at box-offices around the country. Now here he was, standing in

his gold lamé jacket (the trousers had been destroyed while leaping off of the stage in Seattle) and faced by 9,000 screaming youngsters in the showbiz capital of the world. He could not let them down, and for 50 minutes he gave them the works, running through 18 of his greatest hits while gyrating, falling to one knee, laying down or performing an aggressive bump 'n' grind routine. Then, closing the show in traditional fashion with a killer rendition of *Hound Dog*, he rolled about the stage

with a life-sized model of Nipper, the RCA mascot, and left the fans screaming for more, as well as their parents and the police screaming for his blood.

The following evening the police set up three 16-millimeter movie cameras in case another equally 'lewd' performance invited obscenity charges. 'I wonder if they're gonna release this in movie theatres,' Elvis quipped while pointing at them, before promising, 'we're not gonna let it stop us from putting on the best show we can for

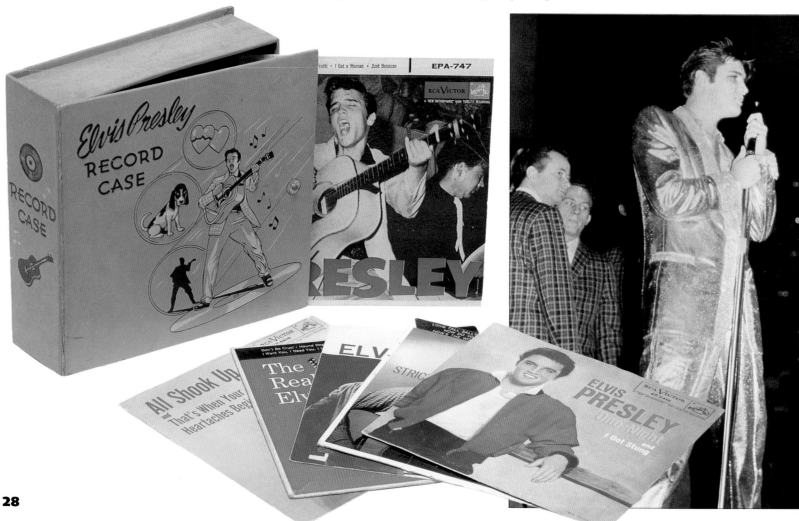

you people. If they think it's obscene that's their problem, not mine... I'm gonna be an angel tonight!'

At the age of just 22 Elvis Presley, the former truck driver from Tupelo, was on top of the world, but within a very short space of time he would be treading on a foreign stage. For Uncle Sam was calling, and while US53310761 was away in the army the world about him would change, Elvis would change and nothing would ever be the same again.

Above: *A collection of original 1950's badges, utilizing various different Elvis images dating back to his days at Sun.*

Far left: *This record case came in very handy for keeping your singles collection tidy, but not if you were buying 78s!*

Left: *Elvis '57, performing in the notorious gold lamé suit designed by Nudie Cohen of Hollywood.*

Right: *Elvis' '50's audiences were predominantly female, while cops and security guards comprised most of the male contingent.*

media madness

A small box, a larger box and the printed word: three factors which played a major role in the astronomical rise to fame of Elvis Presley.

For most major artists the route to success is often an arduous one, and a lengthy apprenticeship has to be served before local popularity is transformed into nationwide - and then international - success. Not so, however, in the case of Elvis, who expertly utilised two of these mediums in order to rapidly imprint his name and image on the global consciousness. The third one, the press, was beyond his control.

Relatively few people ever had the opportunity to meet the man himself or see him perform in concert, but thanks to radio, television and the press, they at least had a fair impression of what he was like... or supposedly like. For, whether the newspaper reports, reviews or analyses were complimentary, derogatory or downright vicious, they

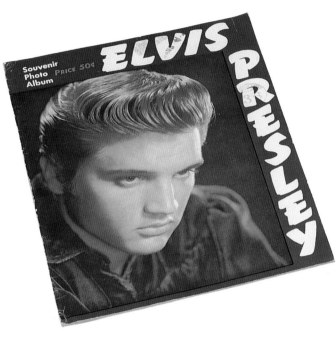

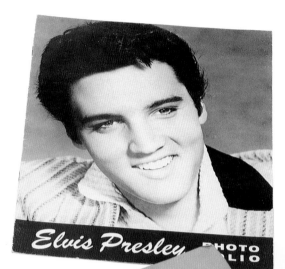

'He can't sing a lick, and makes up for vocal shortcomings with the weirdest and most plainly suggestive animation short of an aborigine's mating dance.'

The Journal American, 1956.

Above: *In the days before video machines enabled them to look at their idol whenever they wanted, photo albums were extremely popular with Elvis' female following.*

Right: *At the height of Presleymania, many ardent fans would hold onto any newspaper clipping, magazine article or photo relating to their hero. collections can be quite valuable.*

nevertheless served to keep Elvis' name at the forefront of most readers' minds, and that was enough.

Sometimes their barbs would upset and annoy him, or even, when the going got really tough, worry him that they could stall his career amid all of the clamouring for his public performances to be outlawed. Yet, in the main, Elvis knew that as long as the journalists remembered how to spell his name, that was all that truly mattered. The rest was down to him and his fans.

So to the small box; the radio, that purveyor of information and entertainment which, during the 1930s and '40s, was rivalled only by the movies in terms of the grip that it held on the public's consciousness. Singers such as Bing Crosby, Dick Powell, Rudy Vallee and Frank Sinatra had all benefitted from the magical effect of having their voices broadcast across the airwaves during radio's halcyon years, and although by the mid-50s it no longer monopolized people's attention in the home, radio was still one of the chief assets in the skyrocketing career of the young Elvis Presley.

It was radio which, in the beginning, enabled Memphis DJ Dewey Phillips to play Elvis' first single, *Blue Moon of Kentucky* b/w *That's All Right (Mama)* incessantly. This in turn led to five thousand copies of the record being ordered during the first week after it was launched on air. Then, with the single soaring up Memphis' country & western chart, the boy singer was quickly booked to perform on that most famous and prestigious of all country radio shows, the *Grand Ole Opry*.Staged in the Ryman Auditorium in Nashville, Tennessee, the *Opry* had been a c&w institution for around 30

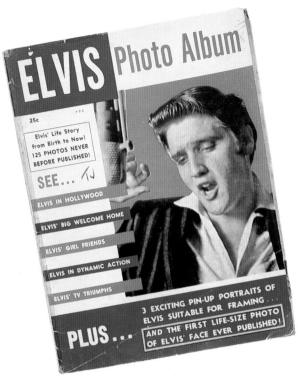

years when Elvis gave his one and only performance there on September 25, 1954. Steeped in the conservative traditions of the barn-dance brand of country music, and fighting shy of the use of electric guitars or even drums, the Opry's 'talent coordinator', Jim Denny, judged Presley's style of performing to be too racy in all senses of the word. Denny actually suggested that the nineteen-year-old hopeful should go back to driving a truck. History does not record Elvis' response to this advice, but what is known is that he swiftly moved on to another radio show that was altogether more receptive to new and different forms of musical talent.

The *Louisiana Hayride*, broadcast on radio station KWKH (and subsequently picked up by other stations) from the Shreveport Municipal Auditorium, provided Elvis and the Blue Moon Boys with a one-year contract to appear on the weekly show and therefore the perfect opportunity to advertize themselves to listeners all around the American South. Initially, certain country stations had considered Elvis too bluesy for their audiences while blues stations felt that he sounded more like a country artist. Yet, as a result of his Saturday night performances on the *Hayride*, Elvis' concert bookings quickly multiplied in Tennessee, Texas and beyond, along with the playing of his records and the broadcasting of hastily-arranged interviews on local radio stations.

Within a matter of months rather than years, Elvis was zooming on an upwards spiral whereby the more his

Above: *An album containing some early period shots of one of the most photographed men ever.*

Left: *The performance that caused a storm - Elvis creates history on* The Milton Berle Show, *5 June 1956.*

Right: *Backed by* The Jordanaires *during a December 1956 radio broadcast of the* Louisiana Hayride. *The way they looked only emphasized how hip Elvis appeared.*

songs were played the more records and concert tickets he sold, and the more concert tickets he sold the more the radio stations wanted to play his records. By mid-1955 he still may not have recorded very much material, but radio ensured that there would be demand for more - and from areas of the country that the small Sun Records label could never have reached on its own.

So it was that radio helped spread the gospel according to Elvis Presley, but then came the larger box. This was, after all, the 'Golden Age of Television' in America, when millions of people would tune in each evening to watch the latest entertainment being beamed direct into their living rooms. Long before the days of cable TV and hundreds of channels, most Americans were seemingly eager to share in the novel experiences that the new medium had to offer, and some shows were so popular that it was almost as if the entire nation was sitting down, tuning in and watching together.

These were the years of Dezi and Lucy, Ed Sullivan, Jack Benny, *The $64,000 Question*, *Dragnet*, *Red Skelton* and *You Bet Your Life*. They were the days of live dramas such as *Requiem For a Heavyweight*, of pleasant musical fare, of good, clean, all-round family entertainment.

Let's take a trip back to the evening of Saturday, January 28, 1956. Over on NBC there's *The Perry Como Show*, great fun for everyone over the age of forty, while on CBS there is Jackie Gleason's variety-based *Stage Show*, which precedes his own comedy program *The Honeymooners*. The June Taylor Dancers get *Stage Show* off to its usual lively start, and then there is the

first guest - a comedian, juggler, whoever - introduced by the program's ageing co-hosts, Tommy and Jimmy Dorsey, swing music idols from a bygone era. Flick over to NBC and there's Perry, smooth and dapper, crooning his latest hit, *Hot Dickety Dog Dickety*, while on *Stage Show* there's... what the hell is this? A greasy, sneering, no-talent bruiser in an ill-fitting suit, wailing about something to do with rattlin' and rollin' while moving like a snake on pep pills? Maybe the executives at CBS have planned this as some kind of a joke, but such obscene antics are certainly no laughing matter to the vast majority of decent-minded, law-abiding US citizens!

Making his national TV debut the day after the release of his first RCA single, *Heartbreak Hotel*, Elvis turned in a vibrant if as yet unrefined performance of Big Joe Turner's *Shake, Rattle and Roll/Flip, Flop and Fly*, and Ray Charles' *I Got a Woman*. He shook his head, over-emphasized with his mouth and twitched from head to foot, and the nervous energy that already defined his stage persona came bursting right out of the TV screens, spilling into people's homes.

As it happened, Perry Como beat the faltering *Stage Show* hands-down in the ratings, but it was Presley's rhythm & blues performances that were soon making all of the headlines.

Left: *Elvis gyrates, Bill Black whoops it up and even Scotty Moore gets into the swing of things during a 17 March 1956 appearance on the Dorsey Brothers' TV show. This was the start, but of what no one yet realized.*

Above: *Moving from the small Sun label to RCA Victor opened Elvis up to a worldwide audience. Yet, while he made many of his most famous recordings for RCA, Elvis never really sounded as fresh and natural as he had done under the guidance of Sam Phillips.*

His second Stage Show appearance featured Elvis introducing the country to *Heartbreak Hotel* with perfect vocal inflections, even though he, Scotty, Bill and D.J. Fontana had to contend with the standard jazzy accompaniment of the house orchestra. During the guitar solo he also drew laughter and applause from the bewildered studio audience by way of some painfully contrived leg-swivelling while smiling self-consciously, almost as if to mask his own embarrassment.

In the coming weeks, however, Elvis' self-confidence grew along with the number of girls who started turning up in the *Stage Show* audience to squeal at his every shake and shimmy, not to mention the increasingly brash and cocky manner in which he delivered the songs. Moreover, his choice of material also served notice that a change was in the air and that the old barriers were about to be broken down - *Money Honey*, *Baby Let's Play House*, *Tutti Frutti*; no longer would black r&b music, performed in the style that it was written, be off-limits to mainstream white artists.

In all, Elvis appeared six times on the Dorsey brothers' show, and by the time he wound things up on March 24, 1956, he had a single near the top of

35

the US charts, an album that had been released a fortnight before with advance sales of more than 300,000 and a Hollywood screen test scheduled for the following day.

The next national TV appearance was on *The Milton Berle Show* of April 3, where Elvis performed *Heartbreak Hotel* and *Blue Suede Shoes* in a style much more refined than before. Riding the crest of a wave (almost literally as well as figuratively - the show was broadcast from the deck of the aircraft carrier *USS Hancock* in San Diego), he was clearly fast becoming the consumate showman. Confident and easygoing, he didn't even allow the

Above: *Musical notes, hearts, discs and guitars all surround the man from Memphis on this 1956 picture frame - made to cash in on his feature film debut - as these were some of the symbols most closely associated with him back then. The signed photo in the frame is one of many sent out in 1956.*

breaking of two of his guitar strings to phase him, while Bill Black, shouting, flapping his arms and riding atop his bass, still attempted to infuse the act with some burlesque-type humour.

Up until that point Elvis had been the front-man in a band effort - 'Elvis Presley with Scotty and Bill' - but when June 5 rolled around and, with it, his second appearance on the Berle show, he ensured that it was he and he alone who was going to be the sole focus of attention from then on. It was a performance that would go down in history.

Things started off mildly enough: a skit set in a record store features Elvis turning up for an autograph session,

and Milton Berle having the clothes ripped from his own back by hysterical fans who mistake him for the real thing! 'Give me the good old Rudy Vallee days,' sighs 'Uncle Miltie'. Elvis looks on and laughs, sings his latest single, *I Want You, I Need You, I Love You*, and is then presented with his second gold disc by Berle before launching into a song that he would not record for another month.

Hound Dog, written by Jerry Lieber and Mike Stoller, was a number which Elvis saw Freddie Bell and the Bell Boys performing a few weeks earlier during his disastrous stint in Las Vegas. His own version, when committed to tape,

would actually follow Bell's arrangement rather than the original bluesy rendition of Big Mama Thornton back in 1953 - full of gusto and aggression, and a far, far cry from the limp, gutless, throwaway treatment with which Elvis would discard the song towards the end of his career.

On this night, however, he really gave *Hound Dog* and the great American public the full works. Firstly, he blasted his way through the number in much the same manner as he would on record, while simultaneously swivelling his hips, firing his knees back and forth in time with D.J. Fontana's machine gun-type drum breaks, and

Left: *During the early years of his success Elvis gave numerous press, radio and TV interviews, but these would be cut to a bare minimum after his stint in the army and the switch to a more remote, exclusive image.*

Right: *A collection of limited-edition 10-inch albums, a format which never took off. The top two were issued in the UK, the bottom two in France, and all but the '60's release at bottom-right date from the 1950s.*

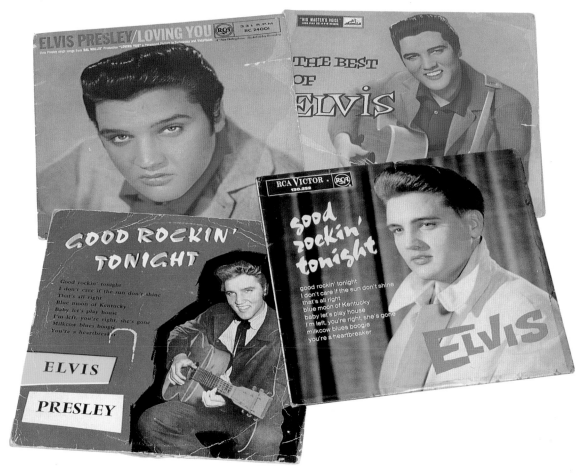

ELVIS SINGS "WEAR MY RING AROUND YOUR NECK"

THE OFFICIAL ELVIS PRESLEY RING
IT'S NEW! IT'S BEAUTIFUL!

An Amazing Value for Only **75¢**

Here is a copy of the same ring owned and cherished by
Elvis Presley. This ring is 18 Kt. Gold Plated, overlaid
with a clear crystal Cabochon reflecting a Full Color
informal photograph of Elvis. The Elvis Presley ring is not
a gimmick or toy, it is a real piece of fine jewelry, manufac-
tured by a leading New York master craftsman who created this original design.
proud to own and wear one to show to your friends. Be the FIRST in your crowd to have one.
These rings are being introduced at the sensational low price of only 75¢ (plus 25¢ for
Federal tax, postage and handling) a total of only $1.00 postpaid. The Elvis Presley ring
sold on a money-back guarantee. You must be satisfied
or your money is refunded.

We urge you to act quick! Send $1.00 for each ring
today and be thrilled with this amazing offer. An unusual
and appreciated gift for yourself and friends. Sorry, No
C.O.D.'s.

ATTENTION ELVIS PRESLEY FAN CLUBS. If you can
use a dozen or more rings sent to one address, write for
special Elvis Presley Fan Club prices. Please state how
many you need.

CELEBRITY PRODUCTS CO., DEPT. P-129
667 Madison Ave.,
New York 21, New York

Celebrity Products Co., Dept. P-129
667 Madison Ave.
New York 21, New York

Above: *Elvis may have endorsed this 1956 clutch bag, yet he was more likely to present a girlfriend with a car or a ring than one of these classy items.*

Left: *It is not known whether Elvis ever wore one of these 'new and beautiful' 1958 rings, but in later years he did have his own jeweler travel with him. Note that the photo on the ring is different to the one in the ad!*

Left: *Hamming it up with Irish McCallah, the 'exotic' star of TV's* Sheenah, Queen of the Jungle, *during rehearsals for the 5 June 1956* Milton Berle Show.

Right: *1 July 1956, and Steve Allen runs his eyes over 'the new Elvis Presley' during rehearsals for that evening's show. Next, it would be back to the old Elvis after this fiasco.*

shuffling his way across the stage during Scotty Moore's guitar solo.

Meanwhile, in the studio audience there was a lot of female screaming amid all of the amused and bemused faces, while around the country 40 million people were sitting bolt upright in their living rooms, eyes glued to the small glass screens. Elvis had got their attention all right, but what happened next sent the public tolerance meter swinging into the red and the career of Elvis Presley into overdrive.

With his band slowing the song down to half-pace, Elvis spat out the words, 'You ain't nuthin' but a hound dog,' while effecting a pelvic pumping motion that left nothing to the imagination. There was audible shock and laughter in the audience and then, the

following day, bilious condemnation in the newspapers and a hot new topic of discussion around the nation.

The general concensus of opinion amongst those moral saviours, the TV critics, was best summed up by John Crosby of the *New York Herald Tribune*, who described Presley as 'unspeakably untalented and vulgar'. Most critics agreed that his performances should be permanently banned from television and confined to the strip clubs where they belonged. Elvis was now *persona non grata* as far as the civilised world was concerned.

But was he? A person of major importance would seem to be closer to the mark, and many producers and presenters were more than aware of it. Steve Allen often let it be known that

he was no great fan of rock 'n' roll music, but in light of the viewing figures for Milton Berle's June 5 broadcast he was prepared to overlook personal taste in order to give his brand new variety show a chance when pitted directly against Ed Sullivan's Sunday night program. Elvis was the hottest ticket in town in this respect, even if he was also something of a hot potato, but Allen was nothing if not astute. He would use Elvis to draw the viewers for his July 1 broadcast, and at the same time avoid controversy by presenting him as altogether more wholesome and acceptable.

The result was 'the new Elvis Presley' (as Allen introduced him), attired in a formal long-tailed dress suit, complete with wing-collared shirt and

39

bow tie, singing *I Want You, I Need You, I Love You*. He now looked like the respectable boy next door - albeit he was still wearing his blue suede shoes. Next, he sang *Hound Dog* to a sad-eyed basset which was wearing a little top hat and looked every bit as confused and lost as the artist, and later on, just to round things off nicely, Elvis even made an appearance as 'Tumbleweed Presley'. For this he was dressed in full cowboy regalia alongside Allen, Andy Griffith and Imogene Coca, in a so-called comedy sketch that sent up country radio programs such as the *Louisiana Hayride*.

This was no great performance, but the whole sorry episode served a double purpose - it accomplished Steve Allen's goal of topping Ed Sullivan in the ratings, and, despite purporting to show Elvis as 'a good sport', it also ridiculed him, his music and even his Southern roots.

So why did Elvis agree to do it? The answer is two-fold:

Firstly, if his manager, Colonel Tom Parker, thought something was a good idea then Elvis invariably went along with it. Yet, while the Colonel may well have been a sharp old dog when it came to making money, an arbiter of good taste he certainly was not, and the Steve Allen idea just smacked of the Colonel's touch. Secondly, as already stated, Elvis was always more interested in being an all-round entertainer than a symbol of teen rebellion - the smooth, old-fashioned appearance of his backing singers, The Jordanaires, was further evidence of this - and so he himself was probably keen to diffuse some of the controversy that was alienating the adults.

On the same night as his Steve Allen appearance, Elvis actually defended himself against some of the media criticism when interviewed by Hy Gardner on national television. The next day, however, furious fans picketed the NBC studios with placards stating, 'We want the real Elvis,' and 'We want the gyratin' Elvis', and as time wore on the star himself realized that he had been set up, and came to resent it.

Meanwhile, back in New York, Ed Sullivan was irked for an altogether different reason; his top-rated program had been pushed into second place by *The Steve Allen Show*! Still, Sullivan 'wouldn't have him [Elvis] on my show

Left: *Ed and El - beneficiaries of a working relationship that gained Sullivan his highest viewing figures up until that time and accorded Elvis some welcome approval from the showbiz establishment. Due to a car accident Sullivan was, in fact, absent for the first of Elvis' three appearances on his show, and so was substituted by actor Charles Laughton.*

D. 103   Elvis Presley

Elvis' Escort

Singing with
the Heart

Presley Press
Conference

Down on the
Farm

Pickin' Out
a Tune

A Show for the
Home Town

Elvis Presly, 20th Century Fox
Serie X
58

Strumming
for Fun

Elvis Presley
Serie N   12

Elvis Presley
Serie X

M.G.M.
54

Right: *Chew the gum and meet the man! A selection of American and European bubblegum cards, utilizing concert photos, publicity poses and* Love Me Tender *stills.*

Right: *The Toast of the Town - in action with The Jordanaires on the third and final Ed Sullivan Show, 6 January 1957. Sporting a gold lamé waistcoat over a blue velvet blouse, Elvis ran through many of his biggest hits, whilst also taking the time to thank his fans for the 282 teddy bears that he had been sent for Christmas.*

Above: *As, during the late-1950's, RCA Victor still did not have its own setup for the distribution of records in Britain, a licensing deal was struck there with HMV, who released the two albums featured above. The one at right, on the other hand, was released in Brazil.*

at any price. He's not my cup of tea,' he insisted. Within a week, however, Ed had mulled things over and decided to give Elvis a second chance by signing him to appear on three shows at eight-week intervals for an unprecedented $50,000. This was just weeks after he had turned down the Colonel's request for only $5,000 per show. Now, however, it was Ed's considered opinion that Elvis had been 'perfectly OK with the Dorseys'. And as for the Berle show: 'I don't see why everybody picked on Presley. I thought the whole show was dirty and vulgar.'

This just showed that Ed Sullivan was a reasonable, forgiving man after all - especially where ratings were involved. And Elvis? He scooped both

the $50,000 and a record 82.6% of the viewing audience when making his first appearance on *The Ed Sullivan Show* on September 9. 54 million people tuned in, and that counted for one third of the nation. This record would stand until The Beatles' February 9, 1964 appearance on the same show.

Although films would help transport the name and image of Elvis Presley around the world, in his home country at least he would never be more popular - or notorious - than he was at that moment. The three Sullivan appearances capture him at the very height of his 'classic' period, and they also confirm something that Elvis had already made plain in the recording studio - that as an artist he was an incredibly

quick and astute learner. Later, this would be also true of his acting career.

On the Dorsey brothers' shows he had sung his songs, shaken his body and that was that; on the second Berle show he had clearly contrived to court notoriety by using his body even more, but still he appeared somewhat self-conscious; yet on all three Sullivan shows Elvis was totally at ease both with himself and with his audience, casually teasing the viewers in the studio and at home by way of slick body movements and sly vocal mannerisms.

In the first broadcast he sways during *Don't Be Cruel*, plunges his fists in his pockets during *Love Me Tender* and, on the last line of *Love Me*, howls those two words, grabs his head with

both hands and looks agonized, much in the style of some silent-movie heart-throb. This is Elvis as Rudolph Valentino, and during certain numbers he has also taken to imitating Johnny Ray by cupping a hand over one ear.

As a direct result of this show, orders poured in for Elvis' new single, and Twentieth Century-Fox subsequently changed the title of his first movie from *The Reno Brothers* to *Love Me Tender*, while at the same time nearly doubling the number of prints to be distributed to the cinemas.

A couple of months later came the second *Ed Sullivan Show* appearance, and arguably the one which captured the quintessential Elvis Presley TV performance of the 1950's. He wore a loud check-pattern jacket, his fair duck-tailed hair was perfectly groomed, and during *Ready Teddy* (one of three Little Richard songs which he covered during 1956) Elvis was clearly having a really good time. He gyrated his loose body, shrugged his shoulders, swelled his eyes, grinned at the band and even momentarily stopped playing during the instrumental in order to peer good naturedly at the girls in the audience, making them scream even louder. By the time of this performance he had learned all of the tricks and part of his charm was that he didn't appear to take himself too seriously.

January 6, 1957 was the date of Elvis' third and final Sullivan appearance, and indeed his last of the decade.

Hollywood was now taking up an increasing amount of his time and it was beginning to show. His hair was dyed jet-black, he wore a gold waistcoat (a present from hometown girlfriend Barbara Hearn) and he was smoothness personified as he seduced the girls with *Don't Be Cruel*, (which he described beforehand as his 'biggest racket...er, record,') and won over the parents with an honest-to-goodness rendition of *Peace In The Valley*.

This was also the famous show on which Elvis was filmed from the waist up, although it wasn't really clear whether this was done in the name of good taste or simply to tease the viewers as to what was actually going on below hip level. Still, Ed Sullivan made

Above: *Of all the hep cats Elvis was definitely the 'heppest' back in 1956 and 1957. Yet, while his name was synonymous* *with rock 'n' roll, it would also appear on country music song sheets. As an artist he was respected in both these musical fields.* **Below:** *First editions of three books that were published early during Elvis' lifetime: a 1957 American biography (center),* *flanked by a British one (left) from 1962 and a 1963 Italian effort. In reality, all three were no more than bound fanzines.* **Right:** *Ol' Blue Eyes and Young Smoothie snap fingers on the Welcome Home, Elvis TV Special, 12 May* *1960. Not only was the ex- Hillbilly Cat now mixing with the enemy, but he was also in formal wear by choice!*

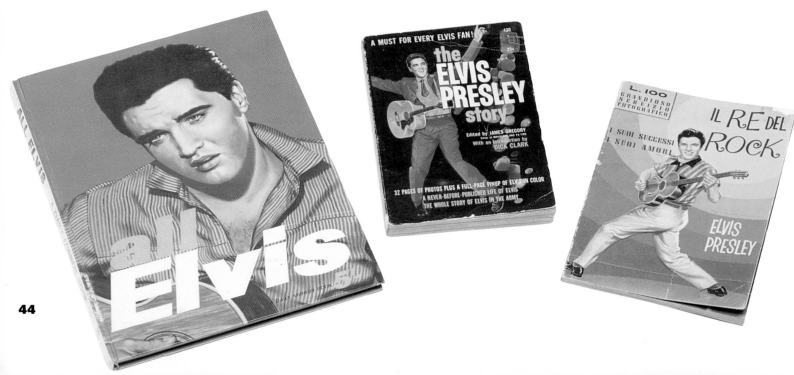

a point of telling America that Elvis Presley was 'a real decent, fine boy,' and assured Elvis himself that he was 'thoroughly all right.' Thus the record had been set straight and from then on Elvis would hopefully have an easier ride with the press and media. After all, if Ed Sullivan said that Elvis was OK, then everyone should be convinced that he was!

Things did, therefore, get a little easier, even though the press continued to sensationalize - and even create - the controversy surrounding Elvis' concert tours throughout 1957. For when he entered the army the following year this confirmed that he was, indeed, 'a real decent, fine boy'. Newspapers and magazines now reported on how Private Presley just mucked in with all of the other guys and didn't shirk his share of the duties, and when he was discharged wearing sergeant's stripes a couple of years later the transformation was complete.

The lion had been tamed, and this fact seemed to be endorsed by his comeback television appearance on May 12, 1960, smiling happily alongside Frank Sinatra, his daughter Nancy, Sammy Davis Jr. and Joey Bishop. For some of the fans this was sacrilege. Their man had gone over to the side of the enemy and, what was worse, the sideburns had gone, he was sporting what could only be described as a heavily lacquered bouffant hairdo, and he was smoothly outfitted in an evening suit, shirt and bow tie that he looked all too comfortable in!

More to the point, however, for that one appearance Elvis netted a cool $125,000 for his total of six minutes on the air. He was now a pop star and matinée idol.

something for everybody

'I want to become a good actor, because you can't build a whole career on just singing,' asserted Elvis during the late-1950's. 'Look at Frank Sinatra. Until he added acting to singing he found himself slipping downhill.'

Well, Elvis was not quite right in this respect. In actual fact, Frank Sinatra did not find himself 'slipping downhill' until he added acting to singing, for his popularity as a singer was still on the rise when, in 1943, he made his starring debut in the appropriately-titled film *Higher and Higher*.

None of this, however, was relevant in Elvis' case. For him, everything was going just fine until, driven on by the Colonel, he decided to throw most of his efforts into becoming a legend of the silver screen.

It was on 1 April 1956 that Elvis arrived in Hollywood for a screen test. For this he was required to act out a scene from N. Richard Nash's play *The Rainmaker* and, as a means of displaying his general charisma, to mime and shake to his

48

'Singers
come and
go, but if
you're a
good actor
you can last
a long
time.'
*Elvis Presley,
1956.*

Above: *Elvis' name
may have been below
those of his co-stars,
but this poster left no
doubt as to who was
the main attraction.*

Right: *Clearly, by
the time of Elvis' third
movie, some publicity
people saw little
reason for featuring
anyone else in the ads.*

Left: *Elvis holds the attention of (l-r) director Hal Kanter, co-star Wendell Corey and producer Hal Wallis on the set of Loving You (1957).*

Right: *Just as a clothes salesperson might say, 'Madam, that dress is made for you,' so producer David Weisbart no doubt told Elvis, 'Son, I swear, this is the story you were born to play!'*

own recording of *Blue Suede Shoes*. 'I hadn't a clue how he would cope, but after a few minutes I knew he was a natural,' commented veteran producer Hal B. Wallis afterwards. 'Like Sinatra and with just as much personality. He's going to be one of the biggest stars ever to come out of this place.' Five days later, Elvis Presley signed a three-picture deal that would earn him an astronomical $450,000 ($100,000, $150,000 and then $200,000), an event which he described as 'a dream come true'.

Indeed it was. Ever since working as an usher at Loew's State Theater in Memphis when he was fifteen, Elvis had fantasized about seeing himself starring on the big screen some day, and just six years later, there he was in Hollywood, armed with the chance to do so.

More than anything Elvis wanted to emulate his idol, James Dean, who had died only six months earlier - according to legend Presley had seen *Rebel Without a Cause* at least a dozen times and had memorized every one of Dean's lines. Still, he wasn't over-estimating his own abilities:

'I would never compare myself in any way to James Dean because James Dean was a genius in acting,' he told Hy Gardner during a television interview on July 1. 'I'll say that I sure would like to - I mean, I guess there are a lot of actors in Hollywood that would have liked to have had the ability that James Dean had - but I would never compare myself to James Dean.'

The Rainmaker would be filmed later that year starring Burt Lancaster and Katharine Hepburn, and Wallis actually offered Elvis a part in it. Under advice from the Colonel Elvis turned it down, and instead was loaned out by Wallis to Twentieth Century-Fox for a small civil war picture entitled *The Reno Brothers* that would start shooting in August.

'I've had people ask me if I'm going to sing in the movies,' commented Elvis at the time. 'I'm not, uh, I mean, not as far as I know, 'cos I took strictly an acting test and actually I wouldn't care too much about singing in the movies.'

To Hy Gardner he asserted, 'If I ever break into the acting [profession] completely I'll still continue my singing. I'll still continue making records and everything.'

So clearly, at the outset Elvis perceived his singing and acting careers as being totally separate, but how wrong he was. For Hollywood is, as it always has been, about making money first

and good movies second. In 1956 it didn't take a genius to see that Elvis Presley had immense pulling power as a singer, and so it seemed only logical to the power brokers that if he was going to be featured up there on the big screen, then he should be up there doing what he did best: singing his songs and wiggling his hips. If, on the other hand, he could also dazzle the public courtesy of any prowess as an actor, then all the better. Hell, that'd make him a singing James Dean, and what box office dynamite that would be!

So it was that the title of *The Reno Brothers* was changed to *Love Me Tender* in order to cash in on the smash-hit success of one of Elvis' latest singles, while song sequences were written into the movie so as to highlight - according to the advertising posters - 'Mr Rock 'n' Roll in the story he was born to play!'

Thus the die was cast, and if Elvis was ever going to prove himself as a serious actor it was going to be an uphill struggle. Still, in those early days he was full of hope, and, according to fellow members of the cast, when he turned up for the first day of shooting on *The Reno Brothers* he had memorized not only all of his lines but all of theirs too. On numerous occasions he also looked to co-star Richard Egan for guidance, asking him about the motivations of Clint Reno (the character he was playing) so that he could better immerse himself in the part and hopefully provide a more rounded portrayal.

The result was a credible performance in a so-so film. In reality, *Love Me Tender* was just a routine B-movie, the post-Civil War setting providing a backdrop to the conflicts arising when

49

PARAMOUNT PRESENTS

ELVIS PRESLEY

LIZABETH **SCOTT**
WENDELL **COREY**

LOVING YOU

A **HAL WALLIS** PRODUCTION
TECHNICOLOR

DIRECTED BY HAL KANTER
SCREENPLAY BY HERBERT BAKER AND HAL KANTER
FROM A STORY BY MARY AGNES THOMPSON

Copyright © 1957 Paramount Pictures Corporation

COUNTRY OF ORIGIN U. S. A.

8

Property of National Screen Service Corp. Licensed for display only in connection with the exhibition of this picture at your theatre. Must be returned immediately thereafter.

57-309

Left: *A lobby card capturing that heart-stopping moment when our boy is about to receive his first big screen kiss.*

Right: *Translated into French, Elvis' first two films were called* Twilight's Cavalier *and* Frenetic Love*!*

Below: *Elvis takes time out to confer with his parents on the set of* Loving You. *After Gladys' death Elvis couldn't bear to look at that film again.*

a Confederate cavalryman (Egan) returns home to discover that his sweetheart (Debra Paget) has married his younger brother (Presley). Without knowing that the war was already over, Egan, a couple of other brothers and a few buddies had robbed some Union soldiers of $12,000 in cash, and now the US Marshall is demanding that they hand it back. The brothers Reno all agree to do so but their pals (led by Neville Brand) refuse. Egan and Paget try to collect the money, Brand convinces Elvis that there is more going on between them than meets the eye, and this paves the way for a shoot-out that ends in one dead Presley.

The fans were horrified, albeit Elvis' ghostly image was superimposed right across the screen at the end for one last rendition of the title song. And this

wasn't the only flight of fancy either, for his leg-quivering performances during the musical sequences seemed more than a little out of place in the mid-nineteenth century setting.

'Thick-lipped, droopy-eyed and indefatigably sullen, Mr Presley, whose talents are meagre but whose earnings are gross, excites a large section of the young female population as nobody else has ever done, and I approached his movie with a certain amount of middle-aged trepidation,' wrote critic John McCarten in *The New Yorker*. 'Unhappily, my fears were well-founded.'

Most of McCarten's colleagues were in agreement, yet while Elvis may have sought critical approval, none of this really mattered to the likes of either the Hollywood bigwigs or Colonel Tom

Parker. *Love Me Tender* was a smash at the box office and that was more than enough for them.

Next up was *Loving You* (1957), the first of nine Presley films which Hal Wallis would produce for Paramount over the course of ten years. In this picture Elvis is a truck driver named Deke Rivers who joins a country band and soon, with his own particular brand of rock 'n' roll singing, is the toast of the nation. Offering fans a supposed glimpse into the life of their idol, the picture has a number of 'in' references and cameo appearances relating to the real man: Deke drives a flashy red and white convertible that echoed Elvis' own famous pink Cadillac; Scotty Moore, Bill Black and D.J. Fontana are amongst the members of Deke's backing band; and, during the scene

towards the end of the film in which Deke sings *Got A Lot O' Livin' To Do* and then jumps off the stage into the audience, Elvis' parents, Gladys and Vernon Presley, can be seen enjoying their son's performance along with everyone else. After his mother's death in August 1958 Elvis refused to watch this movie ever again.

Filmed in lurid Technicolor and featuring several of his most popular songs, *Loving You* was the perfect showcase for Elvis' musical talents. Indeed, the set-pieces for *Teddy Bear*, *Mean Woman Blues* and *Got A Lot O' Livin' To Do* were almost forerunners of the pop video. Also, this film came closer than any other - although still not that close - to recreating Elvis' stage performances of the time and, disregarding the usual clichés and corny plot

51

devices to be found in most rock 'n' roll movies, it was one of the best of its kind. It was also the first of many to reinforce Elvis' image as someone who was not afraid to punch his way out of a troublesome situation.

Right up on its heels a few months later was *Jailhouse Rock*, which, for a variety of reasons, quickly established itself as a cult film. First and foremost, it features the King of Rock 'n' Roll in all his pre-army glory, flaring his nostrils and belting out such classics as (*You're So Square*) *Baby I Don't Care*, *Treat Me Nice*, and the title number for which he

choreographed his own dance routine. In between numbers Vince (Elvis) also resorts to belting a few of his adversaries, the first of whom dies as a result of his injuries. For this, Vince serves a jail term, during which he not only receives a well-earned - and kinky! - flogging but also discovers his hidden musical talents, and once back on the outside he becomes a big star, a big head and, eventually, a reformed character who gets his girl.

All in all, this movie really is great fun, but it is also something of a camp classic for the simple reason that - just

like its famous predecessor, *The Wild One*, starring Marlon Brando - it was so hip at the time that it seems very dated now.

When Vince's gold-digging girlfriend Shelley (Jennifer Holden) pouts and moans, 'You didn't say a thing about my outfit,' he gives it the once-over and comments, 'Flippy. *Real* flippy,' and when nice girl Peggy (Judy Tyler) rejects his strong-armed attempt at kissing her by snapping, 'How dare you think such cheap tactics would work with me!', Mr Mean 'n' Moody grabs her in another clinch and then,

Left: *A colorized lobby card illustrates the most famous dance routine of Elvis' career, notably choreographed by the enthusiastic star himself.*

Right: Yeeaargh! *That guard certainly appears to be enjoying himself while Vince receives a well-earned flogging for being a very naughty jailbird.*

Above right: *In the late-1950's you could flick the pages of this book and watch the dance sequence where Elvis throws his hips around as much as you wanted. These days we have video tapes.*

A prison show gives Elvis Presley his first opportunity to sing and dance.

M-G-M Presents "JAILHOUSE ROCK" in CinemaScope

Property of National Screen Service Corp. Licensed for display only in connection with the exhibition of this picture at your theatre. Must be returned immediately thereafter.

5

57-533

COUNTRY OF ORIGIN U. S. A.

Copyright © 1957 Loew's Incorporated

lowering his eyelids, snarls, 'That ain't tactics honey, it's jus' the beast in me.'

Elvis had not exactly been presented with the best script of 1957, but *Jailhouse Rock* was yet another big money earner and the second of three truly memorable movies which he starred in prior to entering the army. The last - and, arguably, the best - of these was *King Creole* (1958), based on the Harold Robbins novel *A Stone For Danny Fisher*, which, in order to bring Elvis closer to his Southern roots, switched the setting from Chicago to New Orleans.

Under the supervision of Hal Wallis, *King Creole* boasted excellent production values in the form of a good script, great songs, wonderful location shots and a top-notch cast, including Carolyn Jones, Walter Matthau, Dean Jagger and Vic Morrow. Directing was the legendary Michael Curtiz, and the plot gave all of the actors more than enough to get their teeth into: high school dropout, Danny, (Elvis) rebels against his weakling father (Jagger) and aggravates mobster nightclub owner, Maxie Fields, (Matthau) by not

53

only singing at a rival club but also carrying on with his alcoholic girlfriend, Ronnie (Jones).

It was to Elvis' credit that he held his own in such exalted company. Yet, even though his most violent film enabled him to leave for military service with many critics for once singing his praises, in hindsight it also pointed to the direction that Elvis would be taking on his return.

The first signs were in the musical staging. All of the gutsy rock and blues songs - *Trouble, Dixieland Rock, New Orleans, King Creole* - are laced with a jazz backing and performed in a style far more akin to finger-snapping than either leg-swivelling or hip-thrusting. Each number is accorded the utmost respect both in terms of Mike Curtiz' direction and Elvis' singing, yet all of this takes place during the first half of the movie; the second half contains no true rock material whatsoever.

Maxie and Ronnie meet with violent deaths and Danny becomes a big star on the local scene. He also patches things up with his father and returns to his true, innocent love, Nellie (Dolores Hart), and in line with this we see Elvis leave his rebellious image behind as he turns into a romantic balladeer and all-round favourite.

Thus, it is clear that even before his stint in the army the King of Rock 'n' Roll was being smoothed out for family approval - he'd actually had his sideburns shorn for the part of Danny and they wouldn't reappear for another ten years.

On his return to civilian life this transformation was confirmed by *G.I. Blues*, the first of nine Presley movies directed by Norman Taurog and a definite statement of intent. Filmed in colour and packed with nice locations and friendly faces, it unashamedly exploits Elvis' time in the service by casting him as an amiable, fun-loving soldier surrounded by other happy-go-lucky guys who are all having a whale of a time while touring Germany.

Cast as Tulsa McLean, Elvis sports a healthy tan, neatly cropped hair and a ready smile as he serenades girls, soldiers and even a baby in a variety of awkward settings - a train, a cable car and a beer garden. The songs are pure middle-of-the-road pop, and the most popular of these, *Wooden Heart*, has Elvis pledging his love to a puppet! No longer the sullen, vulnerable rebel of the '50's, he is now a self-confident Mr Wonderful, loved by all.

The film was a monster hit and the signs were ominous, but Elvis hadn't yet totally given up on his aspirations of becoming a serious actor. After all, *King Creole* had earned him good reviews, and having firmly re-established himself in the public eye he now had the leverage to indulge himself a little. He was allowed a couple of chances.

Flaming Star (1960), co-starring Barbara Eden, Steve Forrest, Dolores Del Rio and John McIntire, featured Elvis as Pacer Burton, a half-breed Indian who is forced to choose sides when his mother's people wage war against the white community. With taut direction by Don Siegel, the screenplay by Clair Huffaker and Nunnally Johnson focuses on some pertinent social issues and draws out of Elvis one of his very best screen performances.

Less well realized was *Wild in the Country* (1961), a Peyton Place-type soap opera which cast Elvis as Glenn Tyler, a hot-headed youth with a talent

Left: *Elvis was granted a 60-day deferment by the US Army so that he could finish work on* King Creole, *one of his best movies, whose title was originally going to be* Sing, You Sinners.

Right: *A lobby card captures Danny (Elvis), together with Dummy (Jack Grinnage) and Shark (the excellent Vic Morrow), in one of the film's many dramatic, darkly-lit scenes.*

for writing, who finds himself being dragged in one direction and then another by his sluttish cousin (Tuesday Weld), frustrated psychiatrist (Hope Lange) and virginal girlfriend (Millie Perkins). The earnest but clichéd script was concocted by legendary play-wright Clifford Odets, and Elvis once again acquitted himself admirably.

Both of these films, however, only contained a handful of songs between them, and while turning in a profit they fared less well than hoped for at the box office. Next came *Blue Hawaii* (1961) - sand, sea, palm trees, 14 songs, flimsy jokes, plenty of girls and Elvis returning to his role as Mr Nice Guy. It was the biggest hit of his career to date.

Left: 50,000,000 Elvis Fans Can't Be Wrong *was the title of one of The King's early albums, and as a way of affirming this belief a fair number of them contributed articles to publications that dealt solely with all things Elvis.*

55

Left: *Elvis, here with Hope Lange, took one of his last stabs at serious acting in* Wild in the Country.

Below: *As the films (and their titles) became more inane and the plots more ludicrous, so did the accompanying musical soundtracks.*

Thereafter, *Follow That Dream* (1962) told the story of a bunch of hillbillies who have trouble relocating to Florida. It illustrated Elvis' genuine flair for comedy, but there were few musical segments and it proved to be no *Blue Hawaii* with the ticket-buying public. Neither did *Kid Galahad*, a semi-serious remake of the 1937 Edward G. Robinson, Bette Davis and Humphrey Bogart boxing drama. The message seemed clear. It was back to Hawaii for *Girls! Girls! Girls!* (1962) and more escapist nonsense which had the money rolling in.

Following the road leading to financial success rather than artistic fulfillment, Elvis then appeared in a mind-numbing succession of increasingly lightweight movies, all of which relied on the same formula: pretty females, attractive locations, plenty of songs, inoffensive and inane storylines, and often a smattering of animals and cute children to help charm the adults. Elvis would have a variety of jobs - pilot, trapeze artist, racing driver, photographer - and also just happen to possess a fine set of vocal chords to boot. One particular girl would usually take his interest and, despite a series of 'problems' along the way (including the obligatory punch-up with a series of heavies often portrayed by Elvis' own bodyguards), they would invariably end up together - albeit never in bed!

And so it was, three times a year, for the next seven years, with the exception of 1963, when only two films were released. Sometimes these vehicles would be lifted by the contribution of Ann-Margret (*Viva Las Vegas*) or Barbara Stanwyck (*Roustabout*), but for the most part they were pretty dire and Elvis, who looked increasingly disinterested and unrecognizable from the eager, fresh-faced performer of just a few years before, clearly realized this. Yet onwards he ploughed, as, in order to maximise profits, production values fell through the floor and exotic locations were replaced by cardboard sets.

The Colonel was clearly running the

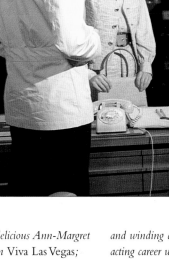

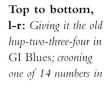

Top to bottom, l-r: *Giving it the old hup-two-three-four in* GI Blues; *crooning one of 14 numbers in* Blue Hawaii; *treating everyone to the* Song of the Shrimp *in* Girls! Girls! Girls!; *horse-playing with the delicious Ann-Margret in* Viva Las Vegas; *playing second fiddle to a dog in* Live a Little, Love a Little; *and winding down the acting career with Sister Mary Tyler Moore in* Change of Habit.

show, and, for reasons best known to himself, the star himself never bothered to intervene. The cheapest writers were hired to compose the songs and Elvis dutifully sang them: *Song Of The Shrimp*, *Adam and Evil*, *Yoga Is As Yoga Does*, *Big Boots*, *Do The Clam*, *Long Legged Girl With The Short Dress On*, *There's No Room To Rhumba In A Sports Car*... titles which matched the films' content. And, when some more time-wasting material was required, old favourites such as *The Yellow Rose of Texas*, *Down by The Riverside* or - most incredible of all - *Old Macdonald's Farm* were hauled in to help.

In 1964 The Beatles' *A Hard Day's Night* redefined the standards for rock movies, but when the group visited Elvis at his Bel Air mansion in August of the following year their long-time idol

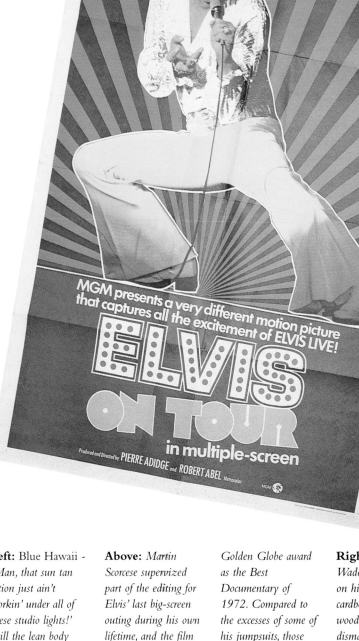

Left: Blue Hawaii - 'Man, that sun tan lotion just ain't workin' under all of these studio lights!' Still the lean body looks pretty good!

Above: *Martin Scorcese supervized part of the editing for Elvis' last big-screen outing during his own lifetime, and the film went on to scoop a* Golden Globe award as the Best Documentary of 1972. Compared to the excesses of some of his jumpsuits, those flares are moderate!

Right: *Cowboy 'Jess Wade' sucks moodily on his cigar amid cardboard sets and wooden acting in the dismal 1969 Western,* Charro!

boasted that he had completed his latest film in just over two weeks. 'Well, we've an hour to spare,' John Lennon reportedly quipped. 'Let's make an epic!'

But Elvis seemed oblivious. He signed a new contract with producer Hal Wallis, and Paramount issued a statement: 'The money involved is around $10 million. If that isn't an all-time record contract fee, it is still fantastic money in anybody's language.'

And, at the end of 1966, the Colonel fended off criticism of his client's films by retorting, 'We've made 22 pictures and 19 have been big box office successes, two haven't yet completed their runs and one hasn't yet been released. If his pictures aren't so successful, how come all the people who made 'em want him for more?'

By 1969, however, even the box office receipts were beginning to dry up, and there were abortive attempts to dispense with the wholesome image: as a Clint Eastwood-type gunfighter in *Charro!* Elvis has a beard and sucks moodily on his cigar; in *The Trouble With Girls* he sports large sideburns, is slim and incredibly handsome, and actually suggests going to bed with a girl; and in *Change of Habit* he portrays a ghetto doctor who falls for a nun, played by Mary Tyler Moore!

Still, all of these products quickly faded into the sunset and in Britain *Change of Habit* never even made it to the cinemas, becoming, thanks to the BBC, the first American film to have its British premiere on TV.

Now, at last, Elvis took the hint and, for once exercising control over his own destiny, decided to cut and run. 'I grew tired of singing to the guys I beat up in motion pictures,' he said.

rags to riches

Elvis Presley's talent was worth far more than just money. Here was a man with one of the greatest voices - if not the greatest voice - in twentieth century popular music, and the ability to successfully interpret a song in almost any way he wanted. With it he brought - and continues to bring - pleasure to millions of people and has served as a major inspiration for countless other artists. Yet, while this should be more than enough for any one man to achieve both during and beyond his own lifetime, it is also somewhat galling that Elvis placed complete control of his career in the hands of a man who simply saw his client as a supplier of dollar bills.

Colonel Tom Parker never really displayed any true appreciation for the natural gifts of the person whom he affectionately referred to as his 'boy'. After all, Parker himself always insisted on being credited as the 'technical advisor' on all of those dire Presley movies, when others with more discerning taste would have steered well clear of claiming 62▷

Below: *It was all very well for the girls to buy charm bracelets and the guys to purchase guitars, but what about Elvis' legion of canine fans - after all, enough of them turned up in his movies! Well, sorry Lassie, but in actual fact these dog tags were designed for use by humans…*

'When I first knew Elvis he had a million dollars worth of talent. Now he has a million dollars.'
Colonel Tom Parker, 1956.

any such responsibility. But, there again, to Colonel Tom there was absolutely nothing wrong with any of those films or the forgettable songs contained therein. They invariably netted a huge sum of money for both Elvis and himself and that was what counted most, for money not only provided them with a life of luxury but it also endowed Parker with the leverage to cut the next big deal.

Elvis, for his part, was someone who had known poverty as a youngster and therefore never grew tired of indulging - or even over-indulging - himself in the good things of life. Being paid millions to sing songs and star in movies while acting as a magnet to women was, as he said, 'all a man can ask for,' and so as long as the Colonel kept the money flowing Elvis was happy ...up to a point.

It has to be remembered that Elvis was an artist, plain and simple, and, starved of any artistic satisfaction in what he was doing, he inevitably became restless, bored and, ultimately, frustrated. It was only when the frustration set in that Elvis began to question the Colonel's management, and it was only when this sort of trouble appeared on the horizon that the Colonel acted on it. For the most part, however, Parker was left to his own devices, having proved his ability beyond question right from the start. Neither Elvis nor his father, Vernon, who took care of domestic money matters, were exactly experts in the fields of business and marketing, and so they were usually more than happy to leave everything - income tax returns, investments, commitments and so forth - to the man who, in their eyes at least, knew best. In her book *Elvis and Me*,

Presley's ex-wife, Priscilla, stated that Elvis would often sign contracts without so much as reading them.

At the point when Colonel Tom Parker stepped onto the scene in the summer of 1955, Elvis' career had been guided by Sun Records' owner Sam Phillips, local radio DJ Bob Neal and, to a lesser extent, guitarist Scotty Moore. Between them they had taken care of record sales, radio performances and concert bookings, until, just over a year after Elvis had made his first professional recordings, it became clear that he was destined for much bigger things and required people and resources better suited to the task - namely, Colonel Tom Parker and the various personnel at RCA Victor.

Thereafter, it was no fluke that Elvis Presley achieved worldwide success on such a phenomenal scale, for, aside from his obvious talent, he was the first musical artist to be marketed in the modern sense. Before him, the likes of Bing Crosby and Frank Sinatra had sung their songs, appeared in movies and continued to do what they did best in much the same way from year to year, decade to decade. Elvis, on the other hand, was adopted by teenagers as a symbol of sexual adventure and adolescent rebellion, and as such his image was all-important. Thus, not only was the song, film and photographic material designed to capitalize on this, but there was also a whole lot more money to be made out of the kind of merchandise which the teenagers were hungry for: guitars, posters, dolls, badges, scarves, hats, T-shirts, perfume, and lipstick in attractive

Left: *Self-confessed nice guy, Colonel Tom Parker: all-round huckster and wheeler-dealer par excellence!*

Above right: *A stiff and awkward publicity pose, clearly contrived to cash-in on the popular image of Elvis the Pelvis.*

Right: *The Colonel and Hank Saperstein handled the merchandizing like a military operation, selling everything from slippers to smart shirts.*

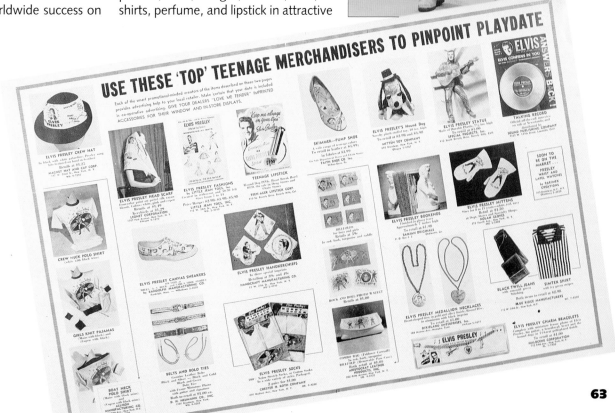

colours such as 'Hound Dog Pink' and 'Heartbreak Hotel Red' - indeed, anything that bore Elvis' likeness, as well, of course, as his printed autograph which, in effect, conveyed the message that the star himself had personally endorsed each individual product. Not that Elvis needed to concern himself with matters such as quality control. Everything was being taken care of for him, and the Colonel, a former carnival barker, was in his element and earning 25 percent into the bargain. Indeed, so keen was he that before and after Elvis' concerts, Parker himself could be seen distributing autographed photos of his client to the fans gathered outside the venues. There was no doubt that during those early years he was a great believer in the old adage that every little helps, not to mention the other one which states that even bad publicity is better than no publicity. After all, being that Elvis created such controversy wherever he went there could be no avoiding the growth of a considerable anti-Presley movement. Still, there was no need to worry, for, thanks to the sly

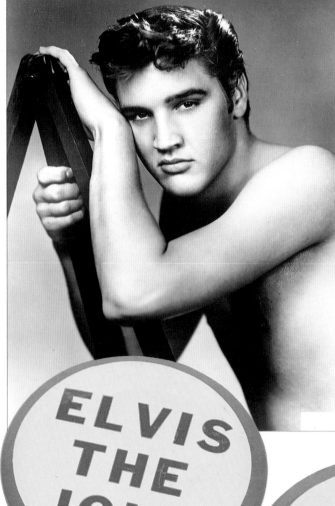

Left: Adonis Presley - an early portrait by photographer William Speer emphasizes the sullen yet vulnerable charms that so appealed to female fans.

Right: Elvis poses in his soon-to-be-notorious gold lamé suit with its designer, Nudie Cohen of Hollywood. Dig Nudie's cool footwear!

Far right: An attractive if misleading door plaque - imagine how disappointed someone entering the room would be when discovering that the occupant was not Elvis!

Above: Shock horror! What would the Colonel say if he saw people buying such subversive items?

Most likely 'Thanks very much!' as it was in fact him who was behind this kind of merchandize.

old Colonel, along with all of the promotional material there was also a considerable supply of 'I Hate Elvis' T-shirts, badges and balloons, and these all served to earn ever more money for Presley and his manager.

A merchandising deal had been signed with promoter Hank Saperstein, whose previous clients had included Lassie and the Lone Ranger, and soon the market was flooded with all things Elvis. But, just as the Colonel never held back in terms of publicity and merchandise, he played an altogether different game when it came to dangling his client in front of the major money men from Hollywood and New York City. According to one legendary story, when a film producer gulped in disbelief at the Colonel's $100,000 asking price for Elvis to sing a couple of songs in the screen version of the Broadway musical *Bye Bye Birdie*, Parker offered to flip a coin on the basis that, were he to win the bet, then the fee would be $200,000 for two numbers. If, on the other hand, he lost, the filmmakers would get four songs for nothing! Not surprisingly, this suggestion was declined and Elvis never did appear in *Bye Bye Birdie*, a spoof of Presleymania which eventually featured Bobby Rydell in the small part of

65

a teen idol making one last public appearance before his army induction. Yet the Colonel's overall ploy worked, for he had upped the ante and there were other producers who were more than willing to meet his demands.

If, on the other hand, a concert promoter made what he considered to be a very generous offer to have Elvis perform at a venue, the Colonel's standard reply was, 'That's fine for me and my staff, but what about Elvis?' The result would invariably be a bigger and better offer, although in some cases - most specifically those attempts by overseas promoters to have Elvis perform outside of America - Parker's demands were apparently never satisfied.

After Elvis' death it would emerge that his manager's name was not really Thomas Andrew Parker, a native of Huntingdon, West Virginia, but Andreas Cornelius van Kuijk from Breda, Holland. This led to the theory that, if he was an illegal immigrant, then he dared not leave the country for fear of being refused re-entry, and that this was what lay behind his desire to keep Presley in the U.S. and firmly under his control. Certainly, although Elvis' family and some of his friends followed him to (the-then) West Germany

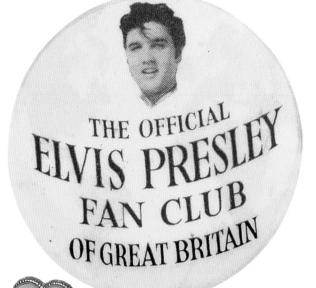

Left: *Even though he never performed in the UK, Elvis' British fans have always been amongst his most loyal followers. Some were featured traveling to see his Las Vegas show in the 1970 film, Elvis – That's The Way It Is, and following his death the club's membership soared from 12,000 to around 35,000. Even to this day they have regular conventions where Elvis films, recordings and performances are shown around the clock.*

when he was posted there on army service in October 1958, the Colonel had elected to stay behind. Yet, whatever the reason for this, there could be no doubt that he was still pulling all of the strings from his base back in the USA.

For most artists, being forced to put their careers on hold just as they were right at their peak would be nothing short of disastrous. Certainly, acts such as the Everly Brothers were never quite able to pick up where they had left off after returning from a two-year stint with Uncle Sam. Yet, in the case of Elvis Presley it appears that both Colonel Parker and the United States Army utilized his enlistment to their mutual advantage - a canny career move on the part of the former and some very welcome public relations advertising for the latter.

Given the power and status that he enjoyed in his home country at the time of receiving his induction notice on December 20, 1957, Elvis could surely have avoided the draft or, at the very least, simply gone into Special Services. This soft option would have meant that, after just six weeks of basic training, he would be allowed to resume his career 'on behalf of the army', but it appears that the Colonel had other ideas. Quite what his motivations were have been the subject of much speculation over the years, but Elvis dutifully adhered to his manager's advice and this in turn produced mixed results.

On the one hand, after 1960 Elvis' career never quite regained the momentum of those pre-army years. He was still big in the showbiz sense - massive in fact - and his appeal may

have been more widespread than ever before, but somehow he was no longer the phenomenon who blazed a trail that all others tried to follow him down. There again, such an incredible grip on the public imagination may well have been impossible to sustain even if he never did go away, for all good things must come to an end. In retrospect, therefore, maybe the decision to become an all-American hero was not the root of the decline which Elvis experienced a few years later, but rather a move which delayed any such setbacks.

As already stated in Chapter 4, there were numerous clear signs before he ever entered the U.S. Army that Elvis was being smoothed out for public approval. This was partly due to his own desire to be viewed as an all-

Left: *Gladys Presley was distraught at the thought of temporarily losing her son to the armed forces, and this possibly contributed to her premature death just a few weeks later. Indeed, in this, one of the last pictures of the family together, Gladys' tired and bloated appearance foreshadows that of her son nearly 20 years later.*

round entertainer, and also most likely because both he and Colonel Tom Parker viewed rock 'n' roll as a short-term fad that could not be relied upon. A change would have to come, and therefore, instead of being viewed as a near-disastrous interruption, the army stint could be regarded as a welcome opportunity to make the radical transition from an adolescent rebel - albeit one whom, we were constantly informed, loved his parents, never smoked or drank, and addressed his elders as either 'Sir' or 'Ma'am' - to a mature and responsible young man who had forgone fame and fortune in the line of duty.

So it was that Elvis' introduction to army life was turned into a media circus, providing the Presley-mad public with the full works: Elvis being sworn in, having his long hair shaved off, being kitted out in uniform, embarking on training exercises, setting sail for Germany, and so on. Uncle Sam was lapping it all up and the Colonel was having a fine old time as well, for he was now able to fully indulge himself in his favourite pastime: dangling the carrot before the money merchants and power brokers.

Having been presented with just a half dozen fresh recordings with which to satisfy the public throughout the latter part of 1958 and all of 1959, RCA Victor felt as if it was being stretched to breaking point. Couldn't Elvis make just

Left: *No longer lean, mean and moody, the post-army all-round family favorite is always ready to flash that trademark smile. The sideburns have gone, but the blond hair will soon be dyed a striking jet black again. Within a few years the sideburns would re-emerge, longer than ever before.*

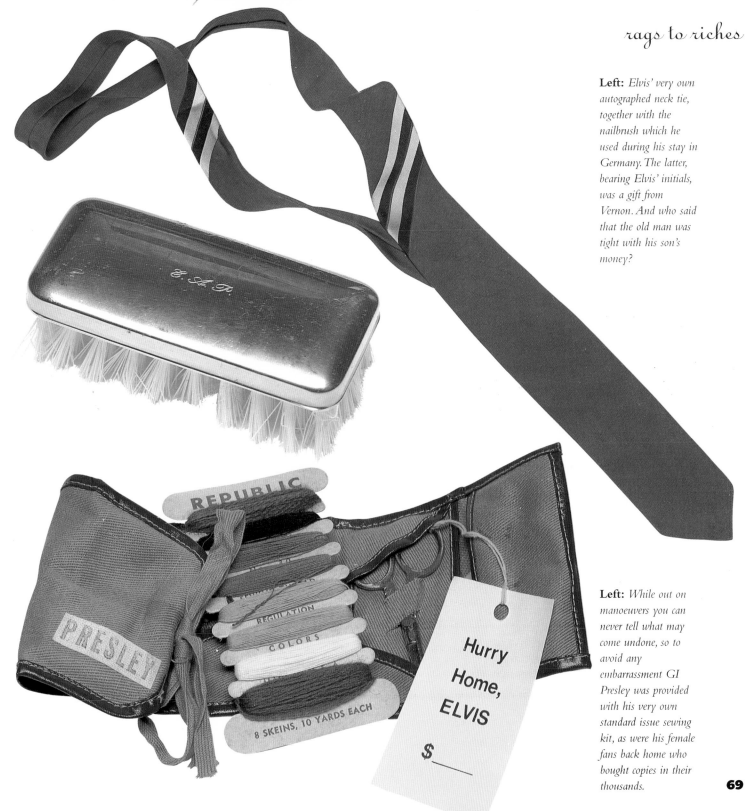

REPUBLIC

PRESLEY

REGULATION

COLORS

8 SKEINS, 10 YARDS EACH

Hurry
Home,
ELVIS

$_____

Left: *While out on manoeuvers you can never tell what may come undone, so to avoid any embarrassment GI Presley was provided with his very own standard issue sewing kit, as were his female fans back home who bought copies in their thousands.*

69

one quick foray into a recording studio and thus ease the problem? Most certainly not! He was far too busy on manouevers! As for filmmaking, this was absolutely out of the question, albeit that during 1959 some outdoor location footage was already being shot in preparation for Elvis' first post-army movie, *G.I. Blues*.

Yes, the Colonel was loving it! All of those big-shot wheeler-dealers who had previously tried to barter him down in price or refused to improve on a deal were now in the unenviable position of being grateful just to know him. What's more, they were close to frothing at the mouth in anticipation of Elvis' homecoming and were now standing in line with their cheque books at the ready. No wonder film producer Hal Wallis once commented, 'I'd rather try and close a deal with the devil!'

Above: *The Colonel has that old twinkle in his eyes as he and Elvis publicize the movie which cashed in on the latter's army stint.*

Right: *The official lamp and shade which fans were able to buy in order to help light up their lives a little during those dark hours when US53310761 was overseas.*

The public, in the meantime, had to suffice with new singles such as *I Got Stung/One Night, (Now And Then There's) A Fool Such As I/I Need Your Love Tonight* and *A Big Hunk O' Love/My Wish Came True*, all of which turned gold in 1959, together with a press interview EP entitled *Elvis Sails*, three compilation albums of old hits, and a steady stream of newsreel footage and magazine articles reporting on some of the military exploits of US53310761.

Fan hysteria was at fever pitch. Absence had not only caused teenage hearts to grow fonder but had virtually turned their idol from a star into a myth, and so it was that Elvis' return to American soil in March of 1960 was greeted almost like the second coming of the Messiah. The Colonel had everything prepared.

First off, immediately after his discharge Elvis gave a couple of press conferences; one in Germany and then another on his arrival at Fort Dix, New Jersey. These enabled him to not only field questions about his army life, love life and future plans, but also to proudly show off his sergeant's stripes.

Next, there was a private railroad car waiting to transport the former G.I. back to his home town of Memphis, but if Elvis had any ideas about kicking back and relaxing he could forget them because his manager had lined up more pressmen on board. Another press conference followed shortly after at Graceland, and within two weeks he was in Nashville recording a new single and album. So much for slowly readjusting to civilian life!

The fans, meanwhile, were soon finding themselves trying to adapt to their idol's sharp change of image and

Below: *When Sgt Presley returned from the army in March 1960, TV crews, newsmen, photographers, 2000 fans and Nancy Sinatra all turned out to greet him at Fort Dix, New Jersey.*

Below: *The cashing-in began within days of Elvis' return, not only on film but also with one of his best-ever albums, released that April.*

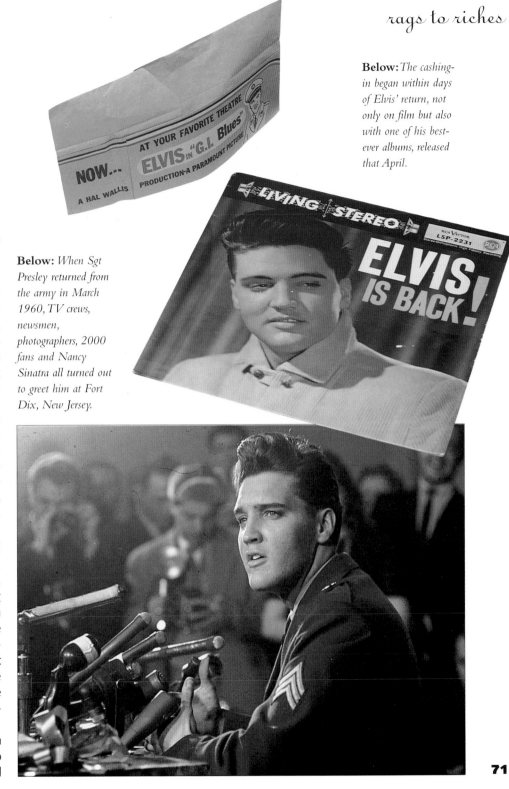

71

Right: *26 March 1961, and Elvis Presley performs in what will be his last concert for eight years, a benefit at the Bloch Arena in Pearl Harbor, Hawaii.*

Left: *A collection of Elvis singles of the 1950's and 1960's originating from the UK and Europe, with their own stylized artwork*

Below: *A selection of official British fan club magazines and annuals, dating from the 1960s and always supporting their man to the hilt, whether in the army or in the arms of some girl.*

people right around the world would be able to see him as often as they liked up there on the big screen instead of on some distant stage.

Parker may have viewed this as a logical progression, but in truth he was losing his Midas touch. For Elvis was too closely associated with rock 'n' roll and teenage rebellion to ever become a firm favourite with the mums and dads, and by losing regular live contact with his core audience he was unwittingly encouraging them to turn their attentions to new stars, different trends and other interests.

After all this was the 1960s, a decade of revolutionary cultural change, and Colonel Tom simply could not buy people off with cheap publicity stunts such as sending one of Elvis' luxurious cars on a world tour in lieu of its owner. Attracting attention by retaining a distance may have proved to be a profitable tactic in the past, but this was carrying things way too far.

On February 25, 1961, Elvis, wearing a white dinner jacket, black trousers and bow tie, performed in a couple of benefit shows at the Ellis Auditorium in Memphis. On March 26, he then gave a benefit concert at the Bloch Arena in Pearl Harbor, Hawaii, to help fund a memorial for the *USS Arizona* which had been sunk there during the Second World War.

That night, kitted out in a gold lamé jacket and backed by old comrades such as Scotty Moore and D.J. Fontana, he ran through a long selection of many of his greatest hits both old and new. Nobody knew it at the time, but more than seven years would pass - and, with them, twenty or so films - before the next truly notable chapter in the career of Elvis Presley.

artistic direction. A shocking lack of sideburns and hair grease, songs like *It's Now Or Never* and *Are You Lonesome Tonight?* and movies such as *G.I. Blues* and *Blue Hawaii* lost the support of some of them while bringing others into the fold, but what really placed Elvis' career in jeopardy was the Colonel's decision to have him withdraw altogether from the concert arena

and concentrate solely on films.

The strategy here was for Elvis to commit himself to three pictures - and therefore about ten to twelve weeks' work - a year, and scoop an annual income of around $3 million in the process, not to mention another million dollars in royalties from his records. That way not only would he be earning more money for far less effort, but also

black leather and tight white suits

1968 was a landmark year in so many ways, both socially and politically, for Western culture. It was a year of change, a year of new beginnings, a year of lost innocence.

There were the violent anti-Vietnam War riots on both sides of the Atlantic; the equally hostile May student riots in Paris against Charles De Gaulle's French government; the assassinations of Senator Robert Kennedy and Dr Martin Luther King in the United States; beads, bells and the sweet smell of incense mixing with hallucinogenic drugs in the world of youthful hippydom; The Beatles and their entourage consorting with Maharishi Mahesh Yogi at his compound in the Himalayas in search of peace and love; and, as rock music neared the end of its second decade, a widespread interest in unearthing the past and rediscovering lost roots.

Indeed, amid the whole whirl of events there was a change in the old pop music adage that anything new just had to be better than its predecessors. The music had been through 76▷

Left: *Elvis' return to the concert arena provided RCA with the opportunity to promote a series of live albums on every piece of mechandizing that came their way, including this rare oil cloth poster which originally hung in the Las Vegas Hilton.*

Below: *The International Hotel was still under construction when Elvis signed to play a four- week season there in July and August 1969. In 1971 it then rather confusingly changed its name to the Las Vegas Hilton.*

'There is something special about watching a man who has lost himself find his way back home.'
Jon Landau, commenting on the '68 Comeback Special.

several phases, from rock 'n' roll to pop 'n' roll, the 'British Invasion' and West Coast rock. In the meantime a large section of the mainstream audience had grown up, and for Elvis Presley, the King who had once blazed a trail and then all but allowed the social revolution that was taking place to pass him by, this presented him with a chance to find his way back... if he still had the will and desire to take it.

Years of mind-numbing movie roles and similarly uninspiring soundtrack recordings appeared to have almost totally blunted his artistic judgement and once-infallible instincts, yet Elvis was nothing if not aware of the predicament that he found himself in. The films were still running off the Hollywood production line, the money was still rolling into his and Colonel Parker's bank accounts, and yet he was feeling increasingly frustrated and disillusioned.

The Colonel, of course, was still controlling his prize moneyspinner and Elvis knew that if he was to turn his career around, for once he would have to stand up to his all-powerful manager and make a few decisions of his own. For a man who had been used to delegating all responsibilities while invariably saying 'yes' to the often half-baked ideas of his mentor, it must have seemed like a daunting task, but underneath it all he also must have known that it was he who possessed the artistic talent and therefore he who had the ultimate right of sanction or veto.

Right: *Bill Belew designed Elvis' black all-leather outfit for the TV Comeback Special, creating the impression of a blast from the past. Elvis himself looked better and sexier than he had done for years.*

So it was that Elvis began to extricate himself from the movie merry-go-round and started looking for new and more exciting avenues to explore. The first of these, in early 1968, was a TV 'special' scheduled for the following Christmas, over which Colonel Parker and NBC had been negotiating in past weeks. The Colonel's basic concept for this was a quickie production featuring his boy singing a cute selection of Yuletide numbers, but this idea met with direct opposition from the hot young producer who had been assigned to the project.

Steve Binder had ideas far above that of Elvis sporting a winter sweater and a ready smile while crooning beside a log fire. He intended to utilise this vehicle as nothing less than a means of resurrecting a legend's career, and to this end he proposed that the star should not only remind the great American public of how he used to be, belting out his hardest-hitting songs in a no-nonsense manner, but he should also sock the viewers between the eyes with some earthy new material. Then, just to press home the point that he was very much a contemporary hero rather than some blast from the past, Elvis should end the proceedings with a politically slanted composition - a statement about peace, love or whatever - and thus dispel any perceptions about him being 'out of touch'.

Swayed by the general tide of opinion the Colonel agreed to all of Binder's wishes... with just one exception: in no way would Elvis, an honest-to-goodness entertainer, be dragged into making any sort of political statement. He insisted that the show would simply end with him waving, smiling and wishing everybody a Merry Christmas,

Above: 'If you're loo-kin' for trouble' - *back in gold lamé, 24 June, 1968.*

Right: *A promotional leaflet for the '68 Special utilizes a 1957 gold lamé image.*

or else there would be no show.

The Colonel had stated his position and that, as far as he was concerned, was that. Yet what he hadn't bargained for was the fact that Elvis had reached the stage where, impressed with the genuinely talented people who were working on this 'special' as opposed to some of the hacks who had been responsible for his movies, he was no longer going to be putty in his manager's hands. Parker made his presence

felt with continual outbursts and protests and ensured that he was a thorn in Steve Binder's side throughout production, yet it was Elvis who had the ultimate say and he usually came down in favour of the beleagured producer-director.

All of this was a turning point and the result, when broadcast on December 3, 1968, was everything that anyone who had ever believed in Elvis could have hoped for. The NBC-

77

TV Special, sponsored by the Singer Sewing Machine Company, featured its star looking tanned, leaner, fitter and generally more handsome than he had been in years. The youthful arrogance had been replaced by a more mature self-assuredness and Elvis' voice was now stronger, richer and even more versatile than before.

The opening was a killer: With eyes full of menace, just like they used to be in the old pre-army days, there was Elvis in extreme close-up, staring straight into the camera and growling, *'If you're loo-kin' for trouble, you came to the right place. If you're loo-kin' for trouble, jus' look right in mah face...'* In that instant the years fell away for Elvis Presley and his audience.

A verse of *Trouble* followed, before the camera pulled back to reveal the main attraction standing in front of a hundred guitar-strumming impersonators in silhouette. Elvis then launched himself ferociously into one of his recent songs, *Guitar Man*, and ended this by belting out the lyrics and shaking his hips while perched in the middle of five 30-foot-high illuminated letters spelling out his name. So there he was, larger than life, the man who had started it all. Never has someone's image been better depicted.

Thereafter things went from great to better as the show presented Elvis talking, joking, and singing his hits old and new in a variety of settings: informally with his buddies and old colleagues such as Scotty Moore and D.J. Fontana, surrounded by a hand-picked audience; in a song-and-dance gospel setup; in staged scenes; and in a concert setup filmed at the NBC Studios in Burbank on June 29, 1968. Another segment, in which Elvis sang L*et*

Right: *Before the comeback: sterile photos adorn the RCA catalogues listing Elvis' recordings.*

Below: If I Can Dream - *digging deep to deliver music that bleeds for the finale to the* Comeback Special, *28 June 1968.*

Yourself Go to a bevy of girls in a brothel, was cut in deference to Colonel Parker's view that it would be out of keeping with his boy's image.

However, it was the concert sequence, featuring Elvis stunningly kitted out from head to toe in black leather and performing on a small stage surrounded by fans on all four sides, which showed the true man, a man fighting for his artistic integrity. After seven years away from the stage Elvis clearly looked full of trepidation as he kicked off with *Heartbreak Hotel*, but second by second one could see the confidence seeping back into him as he realized that he still had what it took and that his fans still wanted to see and hear him. As Greil Marcus described it in his book *Mystery Train*, Elvis produced 'the finest music of his life. If ever there was music that bleeds, this was it. Nothing came easy that night and he gave everything he had - more than anyone knew was there.'

And as for the finale? While the Colonel was still insisting on a rendition of *Silent Night* (which Steve Binder is alleged to have filmed just to appease him), Elvis grabbed at the chance of singing *If I Can Dream*, a number that had been especially written for him. Looking immaculate in a flashy white suit, he poured out his heart as he delivered a musical statement about his wish - or at least that of the composer Earl Brown - for a better, fairer and more peaceful world, and thankfully it was this sequence which closed the show.

The *'68 Comeback Special*, as it came to be known, cleaned up in that year's American TV ratings and gave Elvis the incentive he needed to dispense with the movies and return to the live arena. He had once again touched artistic greatness and this was now the road that he wished to follow. The Colonel immediately fell into line.

A ten-day recording session was booked for January 1969, and this saw Elvis working in his hometown of Memphis for the first time in 14 years. The small but very successful American Sound Studios was the location, chart-topping producer Chips Moman was at the helm and a crack ensemble of the South's top session musicians had been assembled for the purpose. Not only that, but the material to be recorded was of the very highest calibre; an outstanding selection of soul, blues, gospel and rock numbers that would place Elvis Presley back where he belonged, at the top of the musical tree.

In the event, a bout of laryngitis forced Elvis to partake in only six days of recording during January, but he then returned for another five days in the following month and what emerged from those sessions was one of his greatest ever albums, *From Elvis In Memphis*, and three top-10 singles, In *The Ghetto*, *Suspicious Minds* and *Don't Cry Daddy*. In all, there were 36 tracks which found Elvis at the very peak of his creative powers, interpreting songs as only he could and embellishing them with a power and richness that were uniquely his.

Right: *After his July 1969 concert comeback, Elvis was described by one female critic as, 'Thin as a rake and more handsome than ten movie stars.'*

Below: *Elvis adorns the cover of a free magazine advertising the pleasures to be found in the gambling capital of the world, one of the pleasures being, of course, seeing Elvis perform live.*

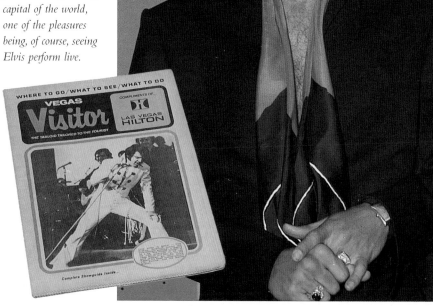

July 26, 1969 was the landmark date on which Elvis took up performing live again when he walked out onto a stage in, of all places, Las Vegas, the gambling capital where he had flopped so badly 13 years earlier. This time around, however, he sauntered into the spotlight at the newly opened International Hotel in the grand manner, backed by guitarist James Burton, drummer Ronnie Tutt, bassist Jerry Scheff, keyboard player Larry Muhoberack, guitarist-vocalists John Wilkinson and Charlie Hodge, pop/gospel quartet The Imperials, female backing trio The Sweet Inspirations and a 35-piece orchestra.

Gone forever were the days of Elvis and the Blue Moon Boys, as were those of The Hillbilly Cat and the Hollywood

79

Above: *Souvenir menus, stickers and place mats, together with the first promotional material for concerts at the International: Vegas-related Elvis memories of the 1970's.*

Left: *Dressed in a customized black mohair karate suit, and backed by - amongst others - Charlie Hodge on guitar, Jerry Scheff on bass and Ronnie Tutt on drums, the King reclaims his crown.*

matinée idol. In their place was a new man with a new image, new on-stage movements, new hit material and a middle-aged, middle-class audience. Arguably looking more handsome than either before or after, he now sported pitch black hair falling forward slightly over his brow, along with super-wide sideburns and a custom-made black mohair karate suit. People were out of their seats and applauding even before the first number, and when this turned out to be *Blue Suede Shoes* their excitement was almost enough to raise the roof off the new hotel.

I Got A Woman, *Jailhouse Rock*, *Don't Be Cruel*, *Heartbreak Hotel*, *Hound Dog* - old hits performed in the new vein followed one after the other, together with more recent ones and even a couple of Beatles' songs, *Yesterday* and *Hey Jude*. All were accompanied by heavily stylized and tightly choreographed movements, and for the first fall of the curtain there was *What'd I Say*, prior to an encore featuring the number that would close all of Elvis' future shows, *Can't Help Falling In Love*. To quote David Dalton in *Rolling Stone*, the man was 'supernatural, his own resurrection'.

Elvis reputedly earned $500,000 for that first, four-week engagement at the International, and the day after the opening night Colonel Parker immediately secured a deal for his client to perform there two seasons a year for the next five years, at an annual salary of $1 million. He turned out to be worth every penny.

Left: Love Letters - *Commemorative postcards from the International Hotel in 1970 and in its later guise as the Las Vegas Hilton in 1975. Elvis' own handwriting could raise the value!*

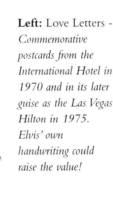

Right: *Backstage passes from the 1970's: The 'show member' one was utilized by the musicians and Elvis' own entourage, whilst the one below was for crew members who were actually involved in the show's staging.*

The documentary film, *Elvis - That's The Way It Is*, captured rehearsals for and segments from Elvis' third International Hotel stint in August 1970, albeit that no celluloid or TV effort ever really captured the true excitement of a Presley stage performance. By this time, however, Elvis had replaced the black mohair stage outfit with a number of rhinestoned white jumpsuits, all designed by Bill Belew, the man responsible for the black leather '68 Comeback Special outfit.

Now the revamping of the image was almost complete, save for the fact that in future the jumpsuits would become increasingly elaborate, with intricate jewel- and stud-encrusted motifs, augmented by matching capes, silk scarves and huge, gaudily-buckled belts. Some of these costumes reportedly weighed as much as 30 pounds, and as Elvis himself grew heavier in

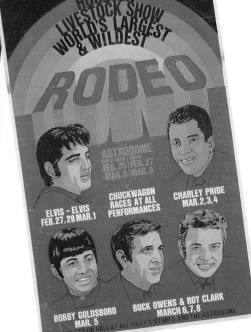

Above: *Wakey, wakey! By popular demand, an extra early- morning show at the Las Vegas Hilton, 1973.*

Right: *A 1970 Houston Astrodome poster, with dates for Elvis' first non- Vegas shows after his comeback.*

weight their tightness often only emphasised his increasing bulk.

Critics and fans alike were quick to notice these changes, but the latter always kept the faith and turned out quite literally in their millions, even when stories began circulating more and more about their idol's drug habit, gargantuan appetite and stress problems relating to the breakdown of his marriage to Priscilla. Indeed, from July 1969 to June of 1977 Elvis Presley performed no less than 1086 shows, mostly to packed houses all over the United States. He had started touring the country in September 1970 and wherever he appeared he always received a reception fit for a king.

Moreover, he began acting the part too, and the formula was always the same: an orchestral rendition of Richard Strauss's *Also Sprach Zarathustra* -

Right: *More than 80,000 tickets were snapped up when Elvis played four sell-out shows at Madison Square Gardens in New York city on 9-11 June 1972.*

Below: *The huge leather stage banner, as seen in the Elvis photo, is amongst the rarest of all '70's items. Three were made, but only this one is known to still exist.*

Above:*Elvis' 1974 letter to an English fan. Note the false name, 'J. Burrows', on the envelope, and the non-Graceland address.*

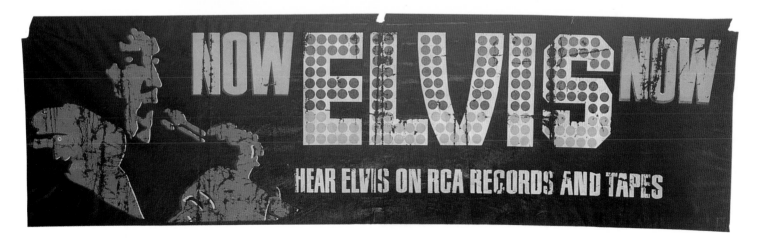

Left: *During the '70's Elvis continued to add to the RCA catalogue, even though recording sessions became fewer towards the end of his life.*

popularly known as the theme from *2001: A Space Odyssey* - would herald the grand entrance, at the end of which, to the sound of giant drums and a sizzling band, a god-like apparition would walk on, strike a number of poses and acknowledge his admirers. Next, he would advance to center-stage and embark on the first number, usually Chuck Willis' 1957 hit, *See See Rider*, and at regular intervals during the show silk scarves draped around his neck would be dabbed in his sweat and handed to a few of his fervent admirers. Then, at the show's end, with the band and orchestra playing the trademark 'closing vamp', Elvis would strike one last majestic pose before striding off, accompanied by his bodyguards, and a few seconds later there would be that famous announcement: 'Ladies and gentlemen, Elvis has left the building.'

While the 1972 MGM feature documentary *Elvis On Tour* conveyed something of what it was like to be on the road with the King, perhaps the best single encapsulation of the last

Left and below: Aloha From Hawaii's *US promo material made much of the fact that it was a live broadcast, but due to TV program schedules the show did not air there until April.*

phase of his career came in the form of the *Aloha From Hawaii Via Satellite* concert which took place at the Honolulu International Centre Arena on January 14, 1973. A benefit performance for the Kui Lee Cancer Fund, it was intended to reach a potential 1.5 billion people around the world by way of their TV screens - after all, being that Elvis wasn't about to do a world tour, this was the Colonel's convenient way of ensuring that everyone had a chance to see the great man in action.

In the event, only a handful of countries received the NBC show live, while others - including the United States - picked up the recorded version some time later or, as in the case of the UK, not until after Elvis' death. What those who *did* tune in to the show saw, however, was the last truly commendable live appearance by Elvis Presley to reach their screens, for all of the magical ingredients were there and, having slimmed down especially for the occasion, he looked superb in a way that he never would again. Indeed, a couple of weeks later many of his band members

Above: *Two 8-track cartridges, together with a 'personal' message (center) from* Elvis, *in which he hopes that the listener had enjoyed the new recordings.*

Below: *Special Concert Edition photo folios from 1974. The top two are both* extremely *rare limited edition items, while the others were more common on tour.*

would be shocked by how rapidly he had regained weight.

Yet another amazing peak in the Presley career, the *Aloha From Hawaii* concert did nevertheless contain a couple of ominous signs: firstly, there was the manner in which Elvis appeared to throw away many of his old rock 'n' roll hits, singing them in a half-hearted manner that was in stark contrast to his renditions of previous years; and secondly, it was noticeable just how little he was now moving on stage, especially considering that the man was still only 38 years old.

Elvis, however, was caught in his latest and final rut, one of overt drug use and endless concert tours, and thereafter - with ill health causing a

Left: *Elvis' famous 'Taking Care of Business in a Flash' insignia adorned some of his own 70's jewelry, girlfriends wore a 'Taking Care of Elvis' insignia.*

Below: *The sentiments were fine, but it is somewhat doubtful that the photo actually captured the King belting out a gutsy rendition of* Happy Birthday!

Happy Birthday to you in 1973 Sincerely Elvis

Left: *Hairdresser and spiritual adviser, Larry Geller (center), watches Elvis at a 1976 concert. By this stage Elvis was obviously very sick and shouldn't have been performing at all.*

number of shows to be cancelled - his decline was both shocking and tragic. Seemingly losing his zest for life, Elvis increasingly regarded recording as a tiresome chore and gained much of his satisfaction either from the visits of his daughter, Lisa Marie, or the contact with his concert audiences. Yet, towards the end, even some of these affairs were but a very pale imitation of past glories.

Bob Iuliucci was sitting just a few rows from the front of the Louisiana State University Memorial Auditorium in Baton Rouge when Elvis performed there on May 31, 1977, and he now recalls: 'Elvis had to be led on stage and when you saw him from the side he was just huge. His face was also really bloated and you just knew that there was something physically wrong with him. This was not natural obesity.

'He mumbled a bit between songs but I really don't think he knew where he was, and although he sometimes tried to move to the music he was so incredibly big that it just didn't come off very well. He didn't even finish any of the songs. He'd get about half or three quarters of the way through them and then just fade off, and so the band would continue playing and then move on to something else. If you closed your eyes, however, he sounded great, exactly the way that he does on record...'

CBS put together a TV special connected with this final tour, culled from Elvis' shows in Omaha on June 19 and Rapid City on June 21. The images contained therein largely tell the story.

Elvis Presley performed his last ever concert in Indianapolis on June 26, 1977. Just over seven weeks later the King of Rock 'n' Roll was dead.

Right and below: *Elvis gave more than a thousand live performances from 1969 to 1977, so it is tickets to the canceled or more famous shows which are most valuable.*

Right: *A torn-off ticket stub for Elvis' last ever show, at the Market Square Arena in Indianapolis on 26 June 1977. The day after his death he was due to begin a new tour with a concert in Portland, Maine.*

promised land

Towards the end of his life, while peering through a window at the fans camped outside the perimeter walls of his Graceland mansion, Elvis reportedly confided in his nurse, Marian Cocke, that he feared people would no longer visit his home after he died, no longer cherish his name, no longer refer to him as the King. Instead he would become just yet another distant memory, confined to the pages of history.

History proved him to be wrong. The first news of his death filtered out from Baptist Memorial Hospital in Memphis shortly after 3.30 pm on 16 August 1977, and from that moment to this the reports, the rumors and the counter-rumors pertaining to all aspects of his life have just kept on coming.

So, for that matter, have the fans, who have dispeled their idol's fear by turning up at Graceland in their hundreds of thousands, year after year, to pay homage to his memory. Indeed, loyalty knows no greater bounds than that of the 90▷

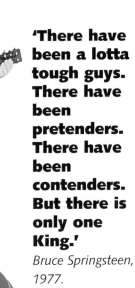

Above: *August 1977 - 'From Moscow to London or Memphis Elvis Presley will still be the King of Rock 'n' Roll...'*

Right: *Belt buckles, such a firm part of the '70's Presley image, were obvious memorabilia items..*

Far right: *Forever young - a statuette captures the gold laméd King at the height of his success and peak of his powers.*

'There have been a lotta tough guys. There have been pretenders. There have been contenders. But there is only one King.'
Bruce Springsteen, 1977.

Elvis fans, for not only has their love managed to survive for so long without him, but it has also done so in spite of the fact that the Presley name and image have been ripped to shreds and reconstructed so many times by so many people. As a popular hero of recent times Elvis is rivalled only by President John F. Kennedy in terms of the character assassination that he has been subjected to since his death, and it is a testament to his timeless music, his enduring charisma and the faithfulness of his fans that he has risen above it.

The drug-related rumors began circulating during Elvis' final years, prompted not only by his worsening physical condition, hospital visits and cancellation of shows, but also by the shoddiness of some of his live performances and the manner in which he would often try to convince his audiences that he did not have a drug prob-

Right: Have you heard the news... *Carrying Elvis' first posthumous headline - the first of thousands worldwide - his hometown paper is hawked directly in front of the Graceland gates.*

Right: *A commemorative tin - one of a limited edition of 49,900 - from Elvis Presley Enterprises, containing series of gold-edged collector cards.*

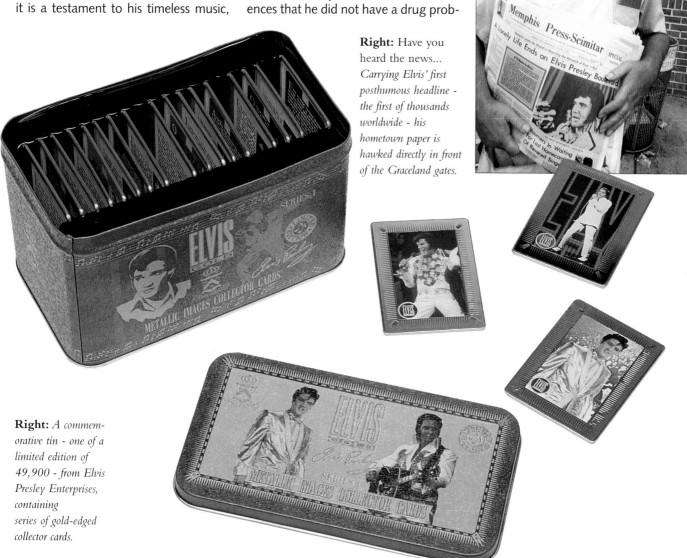

90

Above: *And so the money continued to pour into the Presley estate coffers, courtesy, in this particular case, of some tastefully modest little brooches and earrings.*

Left: How Great Thou Art - *Elvis Aaron Presley takes his final ride followed by a procession fit for a King. But were all those cars really filled with close family and friends?*

lem. Then, just fifteen days before his death, Ballantine Books published *Elvis: What Happened?*, containing Steve Dunleavy's interviews with three former Presley bodyguards, Red West, Sonny West and Dave Hebler, in which precise details of his drug habit, egocentricity and other less-than-complimentary character traits were divulged to the readers.

Elvis was shocked by this public betrayal, yet, considering how many of the assertions made in the book turned out to be true - and allowing for the fact that we all have our own faults but few of them are ever set down in print - the 'bodyguard book', as it soon came to be known, emerged with a lot more credibility than the 1981 biography written by Albert Goldman. Indeed, almost any Elvis book - and there have been plenty of them, includ-

91

ing those by his ex-wife, his stepmother, his stepbrother, his secretary, his hairdresser, his supposed lovers and other members of his 'Memphis Mafia' - would appear reasonable compared to this volume, which portrayed him as a young man with a mother fixation, a dim-witted superstar with only limited musical talent, and a sex-crazed, out-of-control junkie who had to wear diapers in bed. Goldman's book was roundly condemned by fans and reviewers alike, but it nevertheless sold in huge quantities and so the damage was done.

Colonel Tom Parker, meanwhile, was in his element, for before his client's body had even been finally laid to rest he was busy negotiating deals and signing contracts that would

Above: *18 August 1977, and pandemonium reigns as around 80,000 people pass through the Music Gates to file past the King's coffin.*

Left: *In light of the royal profits being reaped as well as the regal image, gold was an appropriate color to use.*

Right: *Elvis' home was surrounded by rolling hills when he bought it in 1957, but this is certainly no longer the case.*

Above: *A tanned Elvis is all smiles at the 1972 press conference that tied in with his Madison Square Garden concerts.*

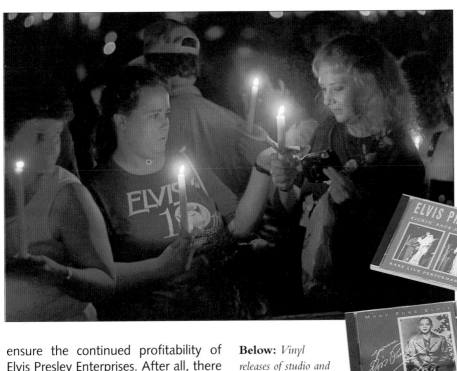

Left: *The candlelit procession of fans past Elvis' final resting place has become a regular and much-attended event on the anniversary of his death.*

Below: *Tut, tut! A selection of bootleg CDs featuring various unreleased performances and packaging that is often superior to that of official products.*

ensure the continued profitability of Elvis Presley Enterprises. After all, there could be little doubt that there was a large and hungry market out there.

Within an hour of Elvis' death, over 1,000 fans had gathered outside the Music Gate at Graceland. By the following afternoon more than 20,000 were crowded along Elvis Presley Boulevard, and within the space of a day an estimated 80,000 people filed past his coffin.

Elsewhere around the world, news reports and hastily-assembled documentaries filled the airwaves and television screens, and with record shops rapidly selling out of Presley product the RCA pressing plants had to work around the clock to keep up with the demand.

Then there was the funeral, church services, candle-lit vigils, all-night cinema screenings of Elvis films - hysteria reigned as the tributes poured in:

Below: *Vinyl releases of studio and on-stage outtakes: Very collectable, very plentiful and somewhat illegal.*

93

Left: *Elvis' death prompted a flow of commemorative souvenir/cash-in magazines, the likes of which had not been seen since his rise to fame in the '50's.*

Below: *Around 2,000 people attended a memorial service in Cockfosters, north London, on 18 August 1977. Hopefully, no one will recognize the author amid this throng!*

'Before Elvis there was nothing,' said John Lennon. 'Without him there would have been no Beatles.' 'What he did was a part of history,' declared Bing Crosby.

Within weeks, membership of The Elvis Presley Fan Club of Great Britain skyrocketed from around 12,000 to 35,000 people, and so it continues to this day, with fan conventions taking place around the world alongside regular pilgrimages by the masses to Memphis and Tupelo.

Graceland was opened to the public in 1982, and now, surrounded by a plethora of gift shops and 'museums', it is second only to the White House as the most popular tourist attraction in the United States. On August 16, 1992 - the fifteenth anniversary of Elvis' death - an estimated 20,000 people gathered there, many of them standing in line for hours on end to file past the gravesite. So much for Elvis' prediction.

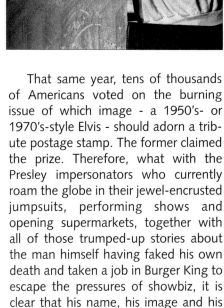

Left: *The pink '50's Cadillac has become synonymous with the Presley image.*

Right: *Symbolism in the film* The Commitments, *elevating Elvis to what many may consider to be his rightful position.*

Left: *Press those belt buckles and hear 'em sing* Hound Dog *and, yes,* Teddy Bear!

Below: *A bottle of delicious white wine, a charming cuddly toy and some very classy perfume - hardly Elvis' chosen legacy, but all very profitable, nonetheless.*

That same year, tens of thousands of Americans voted on the burning issue of which image - a 1950's- or 1970's-style Elvis - should adorn a tribute postage stamp. The former claimed the prize. Therefore, what with the Presley impersonators who currently roam the globe in their jewel-encrusted jumpsuits, performing shows and opening supermarkets, together with all of those trumped-up stories about the man himself having faked his own death and taken a job in Burger King to escape the pressures of showbiz, it is clear that his name, his image and his work will survive well into the next century, and probably beyond.

For, as one fan was recorded saying at the time of Elvis' death, 'Whether you're black or white, whether you're country, redneck or freak, young or old, from Moscow to London or Memphis, Elvis Presley will still be the King of Rock 'n' Roll to me.' Amen.

bibliography

The following books were utilized during the researching and writing of this book:

Elvis: The Complete Illustrated Record by Roy Carr and Mick Farren
(Eel Pie Publishing Ltd.)
Elvis: The Final Years by Jerry Hopkins (W.H.Allen & Co. Ltd.)
Elvis and Me by Priscilla Beaulieu Presley with Sandra Harmon (Arrow Books Ltd.)
Elvis: A Tribute to His Life by Susan Doll (Publications International Ltd.)
The Films of Elvis Presley by Susan Doll (Publications International Ltd.)
The Life and Death of Elvis Presley by W.A. Harmon (Michael Joseph Ltd.)

picture credits

The Publishers would like to thank the photo agencies and photographers who have supplied photographs for this book. Special thanks are due to Ger Rijff and his family who supplied the editor and photographer with many items of memorabilia, photographs, wine and roast beef sandwiches on their trip to Amsterdam. The photographs are credited by page number and position on the page as follows: (T) Top; (B) Bottom; (TL) Top Left, etc.

The Publishers have endeavoured to ensure that all the photographs in this book are correctly credited. Should any illustration in this book be incorrectly attributed, the Publisher apologizes.

Front cover: Pictorial Press; Back cover: Ger Rijff;
Front endpapers: Rex Features; Back endpapers: Pictorial Press Ltd
2: Camera Press London; 4: Pictorial Press Ltd; 6: Ger Rijff; 7: Richard Buskin; 8: Pictorial Press Ltd; 9: Pictorial Press Ltd; 10: Pictorial Press Ltd; 11: Topham Picture Source; 12: Topham Picture Source; 13: Ger Rijff; 16: Pictorial Press Ltd; 18: Ger Rijff; 19: Pictorial Press Ltd; 20 (T): Pictorial Press Ltd; (B): Pictorial Press Ltd; 23: Pictorial Press Ltd; 24: Pictorial Press Ltd; 27: Pictorial Press Ltd; 28: Ger Rijff; 29: Ger Rijff; 32: Range/Bettmann/UPI; 33: Pictorial Press Ltd; 34: Range/Bettmann/UPI; 36: Pictorial Press Ltd; 39: Range/Bettmann/UPI; 40: Rex Features; 43: Range/Bettmann/UPI; 45: Range/Bettmann/UPI; 48: Pictorial Press Ltd; 50: Rex Features; 52: Pictorial Press Ltd; 53: Range/Bettmann/UPI; 56: Pictorial Press Ltd; 57: (TL) Pictorial Press Ltd; (LC) Rex Features; (LB) Pictorial Press; (TC) Kobal Collection; (BC) Rex Features; (TR) Ger Rijff; 58: Pictorial Press Ltd; 59: Pictorial Press Ltd; 62: Popperfoto; 63: Topham Picture Source; 64: Pictorial Press; 65: Ger Rijff; 67: Range/Bettmann/UPI; 68: Pictorial Press Ltd; 70: Pictorial Press Ltd; 71: Rex Features; 73: Pictorial Press Ltd; 76: Ger Rijff; 77: Pictorial Press Ltd; 78: Ger Rijff; 79: Ger Rijff; 80: Pictorial Press Ltd; 82: (T) Pictorial Press; (B) Pictorial Press; 83: Jurgen Keilwerth; 84: Camera Press London; 86: Rex Features; 90: Pictorial Press; 91: Topham Picture Source; 92: SIPA; 93: Topham Picture Source; 94: Press Association; 95: Camera Press Ltd.